"On several occasions, I have had the opportunity to interact with Convoy of Hope up close and personal. Each time, I have come away deeply moved, inspired, changed, and motivated to become more deeply involved in their work. I am so glad the authors have taken the time and effort to share with us lessons that remind us of the power of kindness and compassion. I hope this book helps inspire many, many people to reach out and serve others even more."

—**Dr. Henry Cloud**, clinical psychologist, leadership expert, and author

"The authors are living representations of true kindness. Their kindness is shown through the remarkable work of Convoy of Hope. Through Convoy they feed children, empower women, train farmers in developing nations, and help with disaster relief around the world. Simply put, they are changing the lives of people wherever they go.

"Their greatest display of kindness, however, is shown in the way they treat every person they come in contact with in their day-to-day lives.

"We wholeheartedly endorse *Your Next 24 Hours: One Day of Kindness Can Change Everything.*"

—**Kevin Jonas Sr.**, The Jonas Group

"This book reveals the secrets to a more rewarding life. Kindness comes from the condition of the heart. When a person chooses to live a life of kindness, they receive so much more than they give. Once you start reading this book, you won't be able to put it down."

—**Anne Beiler**, founder of Auntie Anne's

"It's easy to love the lovable, be kind to the kind, and reciprocate to those who have first done something nice for us. Ours is a world built around the bold and the beautiful, the pretty and the eloquent. But what about those who are seemingly unlovable, shy, unnoticed, less fortunate?

"Such people are all around us, and we often take them for granted. But as Jesus modeled, perhaps we could lift up their spirits if—through kindness—we simply noticed them.

"*Your Next 24 Hours* encourages us to do just that! My wife, Kendi, and I encourage you to read this book and to use acts of kindness to uplift those around you."

—**Vance McDonald**, tight end for the San Francisco 49ers

"If I hadn't read this book, my next 24 hours would look exactly like my last 24 hours. But thanks to the authors and the stories gleaned from their combined century of service, my next 1,440 minutes are exploding with possibilities. The authors take the "random" out of acts of kindness to empower us toward an intentional kindness revolution."

—Nicole Johnson, author, dramatist, and speaker

"We can't think of anyone more qualified to share about kindness. The authors reflect what it means to live and breathe abundant kindness and compassion. Their lives inspire us and others to do the same."

—Curt and Nancy Richardson, founders of Otterbox

"We were raised to always be kind when given the opportunity. After reading *Your Next 24 Hours*, we were inspired to look for opportunities to show kindness daily."

— Rick and Jan Britton, owners, Digital Monitoring Products

"After traveling to Tanzania and seeing first hand the work Convoy is doing, it is evident they have changed millions of lives for the better. From Convoy's soil scientists revolutionizing impoverished farmers' crops to the Women's Empowerment program enabling women to live self-sufficient lives—the authors have devoted their lives to wisely spreading compassion around the world."

—Mike Tompkins, YouTube celebrity

"The authors have impacted millions around the world through the generosity and incredible work of Convoy of Hope. Now, in *Your Next 24 Hours*, you can jump into their story in depth, share their pain, struggles, and successes, and be inspired to make a difference wherever you live and lead. I believe wholeheartedly in the work of Convoy of Hope, and you should, and will, too after consuming the stories in this hope-filled book."

—Brad Lomenick, former president of Catalyst
and author of *The Catalyst Leader*
and *H3 Leadership*

YOUR NEXT
24 HOURS

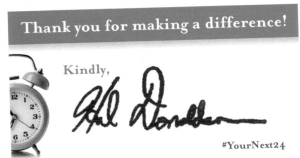

Thank you for making a difference!

Kindly,

#YourNext24

YOUR NEXT 24 HOURS

ONE DAY *of* KINDNESS *CAN* CHANGE EVERYTHING

HAL DONALDSON

with KIRK NOONAN

BakerBooks

a division of Baker Publishing Group
Grand Rapids, Michigan

Published by Baker Books
a division of Baker Publishing Group
P.O. Box 6287, Grand Rapids, MI 49516-6287
www.bakerbooks.com

Printed in the United States of America

Library of Congress Cataloging-in-Publication Data
Names: Donaldson, Hal, author.
Title: Your next 24 hours : one day of kindness can change everything / Hal
    Donaldson, with Kirk Noonan.
Description: Grand Rapids : Baker Books, 2017. | Includes bibliographical references
    and index.
Identifiers: LCCN 2016045123 | ISBN 9780801019432 (pbk. : alk. paper)
Subjects: LCSH: Kindness.
Classification: LCC BJ1533.K5 D66 2017 | DDC 241/.4—dc23
LC record available at https://lccn.loc.gov/2016045123

Authors are represented by ChristopherFerebee.com, Attorney and Literary Agent.

17 18 19 20 21 22 23   7 6 5 4 3 2 1

Dedicated to our children—
may they see a kinder world.

I can look back and see that I've spent much of my life in a cloud of things that have tended to push "being kind" to the periphery. Things like: Anxiety. Fear. Insecurity. Ambition. The mistaken belief that enough accomplishment will rid me of all that anxiety, fear, insecurity and ambition. The belief that if I can only accrue enough—enough accomplishment, money, fame—my neuroses will disappear. I've been in this fog certainly since, at least, my own graduation day. Over the years I've felt: Kindness, sure—but first let me finish this semester, this degree, this book; let me succeed at this job, and afford this house, and raise these kids, and then, finally, when all is accomplished, I'll get started on the kindness. Except it never all gets accomplished. It's a cycle that can go on . . . well, forever.

George Saunders, *Congratulations,*
by the way: Some Thoughts on Kindness

One thing in our favor: some of this "becoming kinder" happens naturally, with age. It might be a simple matter of attrition: as we get older, we come to see how useless it is to be selfish—how illogical, really. . . . Since, according to me, your life is going to be a gradual process of becoming kinder and more loving: Hurry up. Speed it along. Start right now.

Excerpts from Professor George Saunders's
commencement address to the 2013
graduating class at Syracuse University

Contents

Foreword

This world has its hurts and sorrows. And I know it can feel overwhelming to try and find where you belong in order to make a difference. I'm finding where I belong through sharing joy and laughter and song. When I released my first single on iTunes, a rendition of "Heal the World," I decided to donate all the proceeds to Convoy of Hope to support the great work they are doing to accomplish their mission.

I first heard about the organization through my church, which has supported their work for years. Convoy of Hope is truly driven by kindness—they work throughout the world to help the impoverished, hungry, and suffering.

Convoy of Hope does so much to help so many, and they are among the first to respond during times of greatest need. In this book we learn that we too have the opportunity to make the world a better place every single day by being kind and spreading joy.

Your Next 24 Hours: One Day of Kindness Can Change Everything is a must-read for people of all ages who want to be inspired to be kind.

Being known for sharing joy with others has both humbled and honored me in ways I could not imagine. As you read this book, you'll find yourself longing to focus on spreading more joy in the world. If we all do our part, we can—through kindness—become the change that is desperately needed to transform countless lives.

Join me, spread kindness, and choose joy.

Candace Payne, "Chewbacca Mom"

Introduction

What Difference Can a Day Make?

It was the worst twenty-four hours of my life. Not the "long line at Starbucks" or "bad hair" variety. No, this was a real-life horror movie—the kind of day that changes your life forever.

August 25, 1969—7:35 p.m. A persuasive knock catapulted my two brothers and me and our babysitter to the door. We were greeted by two uniformed police officers who had come to deliver a message: our parents' car had been hit head-on by a drunken driver. Dad was dead and Mom was fighting for her life.

Instantly pain and fear converged into a typhoon of tears. My five-year-old sister, Susan, fell into the babysitter's arms. "I want Mommy and Daddy," she cried.

Like a flash mob, friends and neighbors gathered in the front yard. One of the officers stepped onto the porch and addressed the crowd. "Are there any family members or friends here who will take responsibility for the children tonight?" he asked. "Otherwise, we'll take them downtown to the station."

A young couple—Bill and Louvada Davis—volunteered. But the one-night sleepover lasted longer than anyone could have imagined. For many months—while Mom recovered from fractures and internal injuries—we lived with the Davises and their children in a single-wide trailer. There weren't enough beds to accommodate ten people, so we took turns sleeping on the floor.

The Davises sacrificed their privacy and drained their savings account so four children could have a place to live. Without complaint, Louvada spent her days cooking, cleaning, and folding laundry. Bill worked extra hours at the rock quarry to feed his small army.

Slowly, our mother regained her health and learned to walk again. She took a job as a mail clerk, enabling us to eventually move into a place of our own. Our dad didn't have life insurance. Neither did the man who hit them. So we learned firsthand the shame of poverty. We lived on food stamps, endured dreadful haircuts, and arrived at school with holes in our shoes.

Occasionally bitterness threatened to rear its ugly head. But the Davises were always nearby to offer a helping hand and parental advice: "Don't allow the tragedy of your childhood to become a lifelong excuse," Bill said, "because where you start in life doesn't have to dictate where you end."

In time, my resentment over empty cupboards and my thirty-seven-year-old father's senseless death began to subside, and I turned my attention to escaping the clutches of poverty. Eventually I graduated from college and entered the workforce, determined to leave my disadvantaged childhood behind. Earning money, raising a family, and traveling the world became my priority. I never forgot the Davises' lessons of selflessness and kindness—I was simply preoccupied with a quest for success. *Someday*, I told myself, *I'll give back and help the less fortunate, but my career has to come first.*

Fortunately I wasn't in complete control of my destiny. In my travels, I came face-to-face with people who were suffering and in need: an orphaned boy without shoes, a homeless mother clutching her lifeless child, a Vietnam War vet who had lost his legs, an unemployed man holding a "work for food" sign, and more. I could no longer ignore their struggles or escape the guilt of sitting on my hands while the world suffered. I knew climbing the socioeconomic ladder wasn't the path to true happiness and a meaningful life anyway. The Davises were right—fulfillment doesn't come from exceeding others; it comes from elevating others.

> *Fulfillment doesn't come from exceeding others; it comes from elevating others.*

Something had to change.

One day in 1994, I made a decision that would change the course of my life. It began with a couple of simple questions: *What if a person was led by kindness and took his eyes off himself and focused on the needs of others? What difference could he really make?* I wasn't trying to walk the red carpet to sainthood; I was just grabbing my backpack and setting out to explore whether what the Bible said was true: "Whoever goes hunting for what is right and kind finds life itself" (Prov. 21:21).

The impact of my decision was immediate. Like a magnet, kindness pulled me toward spiritual transformation.

With each passing day, selfishness became more distasteful and selflessness more satisfying. I was far from perfect, but I found myself searching for ways to serve others and offer hope and encouragement. Along with my two brothers and several friends, we began loading pickup trucks and U-Haul trailers with groceries and supplies and distributing them to poor working families in California. We didn't know it then, but that was the first step toward Convoy of Hope, Inc.—a global humanitarian relief organization that has since served more than eighty million people.*

My decision was inspired by the Davises' decision. They could have said they didn't have enough money or space to rescue four kids. They could have shed a tear and simply walked away. Instead, they moved beyond excuses and pity to action. They made our tragedy their own and hitched their happiness to ours. Their decision changed our lives and, years later, inspired the founding of Convoy of Hope.

One decision can change the course of your life and the lives of others too. Maybe you desire more happiness and purpose, but you feel trapped, helpless, and overwhelmed. You're running on life's treadmill of to-do lists and unrealistic expectations. The speed is escalating and the slope elevating. You've said, "If only I could set a different course." Well, that's

*Convoy of Hope, Inc. was founded by the Donaldson family in 1994. Today its fleet of semitrucks crisscross America to gather donated food and supplies that are distributed to hungry children and hurting families. And each week, large containers of vitamin-enriched food are shipped to schools around the world to feed 160,000 children enrolled in their nutrition programs. Thousands of abandoned and abused mothers receive job training and help in starting businesses, and thousands of farmers in developing nations receive tools, seeds, and training. In addition, the organization responds to disasters by bringing lifesaving aid to survivors, and it conducts community outreaches across the United States and Europe, offering free medical and dental screenings, job fairs, shoes, haircuts, groceries, access to social services, and more.

what *Your Next 24 Hours* is all about. It's your road map to making this *day one* of a more rewarding life.

The decision before you is a door. But only you can decide whether to turn the handle and venture into the life you always wanted. By taking the first step, you're vowing to do the next act of kindness in front of you . . . until it becomes who you are. You're saying you want to leave self-centeredness behind and invest in the lives of others. In other words, you want twenty-four hours of kindness to become a lifestyle.

> *Through your kindness, you can change your home, workplace, school, and community.*

Along the journey, you will discover that each day is filled with new opportunities to make the world a little kinder: opening a door, flashing a smile, saying "Thank you," letting others go first, apologizing for a mistake, paying for a meal, complimenting the waiter, greeting a stranger, giving a kid a high-five, and much more. On the surface, these actions appear insignificant, but collectively they have the power to change everything.

Perhaps you've accepted the lie that one person can't make a difference in a world where hatred seizes the headlines and anger marches through the streets. After all, the enemies of kindness are fierce, and you're only one person. But what if every person was a relentless force for good? Overnight, a revolution of kindness would dethrone a culture of greed and self-centeredness. The world would be a different place.

You have more power and influence than you think. You might not be able to negotiate global peace treaties or single-handedly stem the tide of hunger and disease. But, through your kindness, you can change your home, workplace, school, and community. You can be part of a growing movement, where kindness offers hope, heals wounds, combats loneliness, and restores what is broken. You *can* change the world by becoming an agent of kindness and compassion.

Your Next 24 Hours is a collection of stories and life principles from people who learned to "love their neighbor as themselves." May they inspire you to awaken each day more determined than ever to be a force for good. Read on—and make your next twenty-four hours really count.

CHAPTER ONE

Ask the Right Question

Carry out a random act of kindness, with no expectation of reward, safe in the knowledge that one day someone might do the same for you.[1]

—Princess Diana

Paul Walker, star of the *Fast and Furious* franchise, earned a reputation in Hollywood for being a nice guy. But even his most ardent fans were oblivious to the extent of his charitable ways. Shortly after Paul's life ended in a tragic auto accident in 2013, stories of his incredible kindness and generosity surfaced.

While visiting a jewelry store in Santa Barbara, California, Paul met a young couple shopping for a wedding ring. During the conversation, Paul learned that the groom had recently returned from his first tour of duty in Iraq.

Deciding the rings were out of their price range, the couple left the store without a purchase. Later that afternoon, they received a phone call from a clerk requesting that they return to the store. When they did, the clerk presented them with a $10,000 ring purchased by a patron who had chosen to remain anonymous. Astonishment gave way to tears of gratitude as the soon-to-be bride slipped the ring on her finger. The power of kindness had reached out and touched their lives.

For more than a decade, the name of the donor remained a mystery. But in 2013, the store clerk phoned the couple and revealed the name of the patron: Paul Walker. "He's the one who wanted you to have that ring," she announced.[2]

According to the actor's business partner, Brandon Birtell, Paul's kindness to strangers was spontaneous and consistent:

> *There [is] nothing inherently wrong with wealth and stardom as long as you [don't] use them to serve only yourself.*

"Paul was the kind of person that valued and respected others. He would go out of his way to do the simplest things—from stopping to open the door for others, making sure he looked someone in the eye when they were speaking, to helping someone who clearly needed to be helped. Sometimes, I would secretly get annoyed because I would see a situation developing and knew my day was changing because we were going to help somebody . . . instead of being where we needed to be. His heart had to give that kind of attention everywhere that he could. That was the kind of character he had."[3]

What motivated a movie star to be kind to strangers when the cameras weren't rolling and he had nothing to gain? According to his family and friends, Paul wasn't enamored with Hollywood or driven by fame and fortune. He saw them as tools, believing there was nothing inherently wrong with wealth and stardom as long as you didn't use them to serve only yourself. He also rejected the notion that self-centeredness leads to greater happiness and success. He understood that life is always better when everyone in the community is better. That's why Paul used his influence and resources to help others achieve *their* dreams.

Think of your heart as a bank vault that's packed with the currency of love and kindness. When that currency is hoarded—it is wasted. But when it is invested in the lives of others, it pays great dividends. With each disbursement, you give others strength, hope, and value. In addition, with time you begin to find it easier to pick up people who fall and encourage those who suffer loss. You find yourself searching for opportunities to lend a helping hand and to build someone's self-esteem. And, you approach each day asking the right question. Others crawl out of bed asking, "What can I achieve?" You ask, "Who can I invest in?"

According to *Psychology Today*, the more humility you have, the easier it is to invest in others: "Humility is about emotional neutrality. It involves an experience of growth in which you no longer need to put yourself above others, but you don't put yourself below them, either. Everyone is a peer—from the most 'important' person to the least. You're just as valuable as every other human being on the planet, no more and no less."[4]

At Paul's funeral, family and friends shared stories of the actor's humility and compassion. They didn't have to fabricate or exaggerate—he had earned every word. And, like Paul, how *you* live determines the words that will be spoken in your memory. A reputation for humility and kindness is not earned by sporadic goodwill gestures or occasional flattery.

You become famous for kindness by investing your currency and being consistently selfless and caring.

Give to others and expect nothing in return. *Nothing!* That hurts. But it's a model of living that Jesus prescribed thou-

> *You become famous for kindness by investing your currency and being consistently selfless and caring.*

sands of years ago: "If you only give for what you hope to get out of it, do you think that's charity? The stingiest of pawnbrokers does that" (Luke 6:34). On the surface, when you give freely of your time and resources, receiving nothing in return can appear absolutely inequitable. But if you're playing life's long game, then receiving nothing is a noble pursuit filled with lasting dividends. Hall of Fame basketball coach John Wooden put it this way: "You can't live a perfect day without doing something for someone who will never be able to repay you."[5]

Many have adopted this same philosophy, choosing to offer assistance to others without regard for personal gain, publicity, or self-promotion. Actor Jake Gyllenhaal, for example, was shopping in Beverly Hills when he noticed a row of parking meters had expired. Drivers were on the verge of earning citations from a police officer when Jake took action. He hurriedly dug into his pockets for quarters and proceeded to top off the meters.[6] The episode only became news when an eyewitness reported it to a tabloid.

Amy Adams is another actor who seized an opportunity to do something kind. While boarding a commercial airline, she noticed a soldier in uniform on her flight. Quietly she approached her fellow passenger, saying, "Sir, thank you for your service—I'd like you to take my seat in first class."

Asked about it later by a reporter, Amy said, "I didn't do it to bring attention to myself—I did it to express appreciation to our troops."[7]

Actor Keanu Reeves's spontaneous act of kindness on the New York City subway was captured on video and posted on YouTube. When an exasperated female passenger entered the crowded car hoisting a large duffel bag, Reeves immediately motioned for her to take his seat. The woman smiled and nodded her appreciation without realizing the identity of her benefactor.[8]

Jake, Amy, and Keanu were motivated by what they could give—not by what they could get. But when you follow their example and give to others, you may receive more benefit than you realize. Researchers have discovered that kindness—and investing in others—can influence the quality and longevity of a person's life. In his TED talk, "Why Leaders Eat Last," author Simon Sinek said a study of the brain chemical oxytocin showed that doing, seeing, and receiving acts of kindness release oxytocin in the brain, which boosts the immune system and makes humans feel happier. "Remember, our bodies are trying to get us to repeat behaviors that are in our best interest. And it's making us feel good when we see . . . acts of human generosity so that *we* will [also] do them. In fact, the more Oxytocin you have in your body, the more generous you actually become."[9]

A study by the National Academy of Sciences revealed that happier people live 35 percent longer.[10] Kindness *is* your ticket to health and happiness. It's the price of admission to a new and exciting world filled with greater purpose and contentment. You hold the ticket in your hand—it's up to you whether you use it. Don't allow your quest for success to

*Personal achievement brings temporary satisfaction; helping others achieve **their** dreams yields lasting fulfillment.*

hold you back. Because, as Paul Walker discovered, true success isn't measured by what you achieve or how much you accumulate. It's largely defined by what you do for others. The daily struggle to accomplish more for yourself won't lead to greater happiness anyway. Personal achievement brings temporary satisfaction; helping others achieve *their* dreams yields lasting fulfillment.

Today you can cash in your ticket to health and happiness by simply asking the right question: "Who can I invest in?"

KIND WAYS

1. Use social media to track people's birthdays and send them emails of appreciation on their special day.
2. Offer to care for someone's pet when the owner is out of town.
3. Sweep the walkway, rake the leaves, or shovel the snow for neighbors while they are at work or away for the weekend.
4. Organize a group of friends to pick up litter in your town.
5. Leave a note of gratitude for your server in a restaurant.

CHAPTER TWO

Get Off Your Own Back

Your time is limited, so don't waste it living someone else's life. Don't be trapped by . . . living with the results of other people's thinking. Don't let the noise of others' opinions drown out your own inner voice. And most importantly, have the courage to follow your heart and intuition. [1]

—Steve Jobs

Before Kate Winslet became an Academy Award winner, she had to learn to admire her body and be kind to herself. The star of such films as *Titanic, Divergent*, and *Steve Jobs*, she grew up running from bullies. Day after day, she felt the sting of their insults because she was "chubby" and couldn't afford fashionable clothes or the latest hairstyle. Cruel words and childish pranks chipped away at her self-esteem. For years, she suffered from feelings of inferiority.

"I never heard positive reinforcement about my body image from any female in my life," Kate admitted on an episode of *Running Wild with Bear Grylls*. "I only heard negatives.

That's very damaging because then you're programmed as a young woman to immediately scrutinize yourself and how you look."

Kate now works to inspire girls—including her own daughter—to embrace who they are regardless of their size or station in life. She also took a stand against Madison Avenue, refusing to allow advertisers and magazines to airbrush her photographs. "The retouching is excessive," she said. "I do not look like that and, more importantly, I don't desire to look like that."[2]

To combat stereotypes, Kate regularly practices a self-esteem exercise with her young daughter: "I stand in front of the mirror and say to Mia, 'We are so lucky we have a shape. We're so lucky that we're curvy. We're so lucky that we've got good bums.' And she'll say, 'Mummy, I know—thank God.'"[3]

If *your* self-esteem has been injured, go to a mirror right now and tell yourself, "I may not be *People* magazine's 'Sexiest Person Alive'—but I am special. I have something unique to offer the world." The more love you have for yourself, the more love you have to give away. It's easy to obsess over your perceived shortcomings, but they aren't real. The bar you set for yourself should be based on your unique qualities and talents—not those belonging to someone else. Who said the best version of you required the figure of Heidi Klum, the fame of Jennifer Lawrence, the athletic grace of Stephen Curry, or the business smarts of Bill Gates? You have a unique capacity to bring hope and beauty to the world. Don't waste your precious energy using the wrong ruler.

> *The more love you have for yourself, the more love you have to give away.*

Granted, not everyone will acknowledge your unique gifts. But don't allow how others see you to dictate how you see yourself. The words they use to describe you don't define you. You can't control how they respond to you, but you can influence what they have to respond to. So, what are you showing them? Sadness or joy? Greed or generosity? Apathy or kindness? What do your facial expressions and words convey about how you view yourself? If you tell yourself you're ugly, untalented, and unlovable, you're probably sending that same message to others.

Motivational speaker Brian Tracey says, "The more you like and respect yourself, the more you like and respect other people. The more you consider yourself to be a valuable and worthwhile person, the more you consider others to be valuable and worthwhile as well. The more you accept yourself just as you are, the more you accept others just as they are."[4]

If you've been wounded by friends or family—or through insensitive remarks or blatant attacks—you're not alone. Millions live with secret pain. Bitterness has stolen their dreams and buried their talents. But you can reject that outcome. You have the power to break free from anger and resentment and to set a new course for your life. Don't fix your eyes on your past; fix them on what you can become.

Here's a simple exercise you can do to launch a fresh start. Get two index cards or sheets of paper. Label one "Card of Lies" and write out a list of the lies that have held you back. Label the other "Card of Truth" and substitute the lies with truths. Kate, for example, replaced "you're chubby" with "you're beautifully curvy."

Once you have two lists, tear the "Card of Lies" into tiny pieces and throw it in the garbage or fireplace. Then take the "Card of Truth" and tape it to your bathroom mirror to remind you of the new reality you've chosen to accept. It's time to leave the lies behind and embrace your new and promising future.

Here are ten ways you can be kind to yourself:

1. *Don't look back.* Renowned architect Frank Lloyd Wright designed magnificent structures. Toward the end of his career, a reporter asked, "Of all your many beautiful designs, which one is your favorite?" Wright replied, "My next one."[5] You will face obstacles and hardships, but make a decision that you're going to press on beyond life's disappointments and challenges. There's no need to revisit the "Card of Lies." Life's windshield is large and the rearview mirror is small— because what is in front of you is far more important than what is behind you. What you dwell on determines your destination and destiny. Mahatma Gandhi said, "Man often becomes what he believes himself to be."[6]

2. *Encourage yourself.* Throughout the day, give yourself pep talks. Build yourself up rather than tear yourself down. When the weight of the world is on your shoulders, get off your own back!

3. *Spread optimism.* Television legend Fred Rogers said positivity is a form of kindness: "If only you could sense how important you are to the lives of those you meet; how important you can be to people you may never even dream of. There is something of yourself that you leave at every meeting with another person."[7]

4. *Forgive yourself and others.* Harboring guilt and bitterness is like allowing a weed to grow in your front

yard. One of the best ways to be kind to yourself is to pull that weed out by the root so it never grows back. In his book *Enemies of the Heart*, Andy Stanley wrote, "Forgiveness is merely a gift from one undeserving soul to another. Forgiveness is the gift that ensures my freedom from a prison of bitterness and resentment."[8]

5. *Be a peacemaker.* Conflict is inevitable, but it doesn't have to create permanent disunity and disharmony. Keep your stress level low by overlooking minor matters and giving others the benefit of the doubt. Albert Schweitzer said, "Constant kindness can accomplish much. [Just] as the sun makes ice melt, kindness causes misunderstanding, mistrust and hostility to evaporate."[9]

> *Make it a routine to look at your reflection and say, "I love the person God made me."*

6. *Remain healthy.* Be kind to yourself by getting adequate rest, eating right, exercising regularly, and taking time each day to just be with you.

7. *Surround yourself with the right people.* Nurture friendships with people who will tell you the truth, guard your back, and offer fresh perspective. Minimize the influence of petty and passive-aggressive "friends" by not inviting them into your inner circle.

8. *Learn to be content.* Often people are unhappy, unfulfilled, and chronically anxious because they believe the grass is greener elsewhere. They tell themselves life would be more fulfilling with a new relationship, different job, better apartment, or nicer car. In the Bible, an imprisoned follower of Jesus wrote, "I have learned to be content whatever the circumstances" (Phil. 4:11 NIV).

9. *Celebrate others' success.* Besides serving others, also look for opportunities to honor their achievements.

10. *Smile in the mirror.* Make it a routine to look at your reflection and say, "I love the person God made me."

In your quest to assist others, invest in yourself. Be careful not to ignore your own physical, emotional, and spiritual needs while serving others. Find a balance between helping others and taking care of yourself. You won't be investing in anyone if you're chronically fatigued or emotionally spent. The airlines have it right when they instruct passengers, in the event of an emergency, to put the oxygen mask on themselves first. Your well-being is essential to the well-being of others.

Vacations, date nights, exercise, and reading are great ways to incentivize and rejuvenate your heart and mind.

When media mogul Ted Turner was asked for the key to his success, he replied, "Leisure time."[10] What have you done for yourself lately? What are you looking forward to? Vacations, date nights, exercise, and reading are great ways to incentivize and rejuvenate your heart and mind.

Investing in yourself will pay dividends for you and others. Author Erwin McManus said, "Decide now that there's a day coming where the world's going to need you at the highest level of competency. Decide now that the world needs you exercising at the highest level of your talent, and skill, and intellect. Stop coasting through life because life is easy. Act as if a challenge is coming and you will be needed at your best."[11]

Today, move beyond the obstacles, stereotypes, and lies that have kept you from being "at your best." Tiptoe if you must, but take the first steps toward being kind to others by being kind to yourself.

KIND WAYS

1. Keep a journal in which you record your daily blessings.
2. Take at least a fifteen-minute walk alone each day.
3. Create a "bucket list" of things you want to experience and places you want to go.
4. De-clutter your life by cleaning your house and organizing your files.
5. Reduce your stress level by following a financial plan.

CHAPTER THREE

Be Their Miracle

There's more to life than basketball. The most important
thing is . . . taking care of each other and loving each other
no matter what.[1]

—Stephen Curry

Each evening New York's Jorge Munoz wheels his pickup
to one of Queens' grittier corners. There, dozens of day
laborers, homeless, and hungry men step from the shadows
and gather around Jorge's tailgate, where he serves home-
cooked meals, coffee, hot chocolate, and healthy doses of
encouragement.

What the recipients don't know is that Jorge is not a rich
man. Nor is he self-employed. He's a full-time school bus
driver who relies on his family's limited resources to deliver
one hundred fifty meals nightly, 365 days a year.

The family buys the food in bulk and stores it in their
tiny dining room. Each day, before heading to work, Jorge
awakens early to prepare the meals. "It's a beautiful thing,"

YOUR NEXT 24 HOURS

he said, "to hand someone a meal who hasn't eaten all day and that person looks at you and says, 'Thanks so much— God bless you!'"[2]

For Jorge, kindness is simply helping others by doing what you can with what you have. Some people are reluctant to extend a helping hand because they're so focused on what they don't have: the house isn't big enough, the car isn't nice enough, and the bank account isn't fat enough. But if they were to take inventory of their time and resources, they'd discover they actually have plenty to share. They don't have to wait until they win the lottery to show kindness. They need to simply ask, "What *can* I do right now?" What if Jorge had waited until he could afford to serve filet mignon or remodel his kitchen? There would be one hundred fifty more hungry stomachs tonight and fifty thousand more each year.

> *Kindness is simply helping others by doing what you can with what you have.*

One of the most remarkable moments in history occurred when five thousand people gathered in a remote area to hear Jesus speak. As evening fell it was suggested the crowd be dispersed to go find food. But Jesus challenged his team to feed them. Bewildered, the team collected all the food they had on hand—five loaves of bread and two fish. Naturally they assumed that wasn't enough, but little did they know that the bread and fish were the starting point for a supersized miracle. Jesus multiplied their paltry buffet into a massive feast.

You may be taking inventory of your own assets and telling yourself, *I have so little to give and it's not even worth the effort.* But your generosity and means—no matter how meager—could be the starting point of someone else's miracle. When you and others share what *you* have, many receive what they *don't* have.

Your resourcefulness is a valuable resource! Look outside the box. Be creative. Assess what you really have and find a way to use it for good. If all you possess are two hands, collect trash along the way. If all you own is a smile, use it to befriend someone who is lonely. If all you have is an umbrella, share it with someone who's quivering in the rain. If all you have is a kind word, encourage those who think the world is against them. To the lonely, rain-soaked, and downtrodden, your resourcefulness is their miracle.

> *When you and others share what you have, many receive what they don't have.*

Creativity and resourcefulness are often powerful expressions of kindness. Children in Africa receive nutritious food and clean drinking water because someone had a new idea. Drug addicts in New York City are rehabilitated because someone tried a fresh approach. Children at a local elementary school have new computers because someone launched a fund-raiser. Like Jorge, begin thinking creatively about what you can do to meet a need or to gather assets to benefit others. You may be surprised by all the good that can be accomplished when you look outside the box.

When the following three citizens encountered a need, they chose not to look away as if it didn't exist. Instead, they asked, "What can I do?" Their resourcefulness became the solution to someone's problem.

In Michigan, a man asked what he could do to help a young, unemployed stranger. When the two met, the young man confessed that he was struggling to keep food on the table for his wife and three children. After some discussion, the older man and his wife agreed on a solution: in his early sixties, he decided to submit the paperwork for early retirement and make it possible for the stranger to assume *his* job.[3]

A Kentucky teenager came upon a stranded motorist who had locked his key and cell phone in his car. The teenager, who was riding a bicycle, saw the driver kick a tire in frustration. "What's wrong?" the boy asked. The driver explained that his family only had one car, so his wife had no way of coming to his rescue. Thinking quickly, the youth handed the man his cell phone. "Call your wife and tell her I'm coming to get the extra key." The driver replied, "That's a seven-mile bike trip." The boy smiled and nodded. "Don't worry—I need the exercise," he said.[4]

A Dallas woman found a way to help a deflated grocery clerk named Sherry. With an ice storm approaching, the store was packed with patrons purchasing emergency supplies. One middle-aged woman in the checkout line asked Sherry how her evening was going. "Not very well," the young woman answered frankly. She proceeded to explain that her car window was broken and she was afraid the plastic protection would not hold up, especially since she was working the swing shift. "Well, I hope your evening gets better," the customer said before exiting the store and embarking on a mission of her own. With sleet falling, she marched across the parking lot to a bank. She convinced the bank manager to close one of his drive-thru lanes so Sherry could park her car under the canopy. Returning to the store, she asked the manager to give Sherry a short break so she could repark her car. A stunned Sherry smiled and said, "Thank you," but the customer wasn't looking for a standing ovation. Heading for the door, she simply turned and said, "Have a nice evening."[5]

Kindness and ingenuity cannot solve every social problem. Obviously some issues require resources, cooperation, and hard work. It's become convenient to blame problems on insufficient funding, but often the cause is much deeper. Many challenges go

They underestimate their potential as problem solvers and misjudge the assets at their disposal.

unmet because citizens aren't asking, "What do I have?" and "What can I do?" They underestimate their potential as problem solvers and misjudge the assets at their disposal. Consequently, problems persist and people don't receive the help they need. If only more citizens could find the courage to try, they would be a fountain of ideas and a waterfall of good deeds.

You're reading this book, in part, because you want to make a difference in the lives of other people. You want to see a movement of kindness transform your community and the world. You want less crime and conflict—and more hope and compassion. But that will only happen if people like you move beyond security to action. Sure, you can play it safe. Lots of people do. You can doubt your abilities, question your assets, and choose to do nothing. But that won't change the world. That won't even change you. Like Jorge, step out and take a risk—do what you can with what you have. Believe in yourself and become someone's miracle.

KIND WAYS

1. Identify an eyesore in the community and get permission to give it a fresh coat of paint.

2. Participate in a drive to collect backpacks and school supplies for underprivileged kids.
3. Help a young person from a poorer family earn his or her first car.
4. Organize a neighborhood garage sale and use the proceeds to help abused women and children.
5. Recruit your friends to conduct a book drive for your local library.

CHAPTER FOUR

When Less Is More

I must be willing to give whatever it takes to do good to others.
This requires that I be willing to give until it hurts.[1]

—Mother Teresa

Have you ever thought about giving your coffee money to a hungry stranger? How about your kidney? That was the sacrifice made by Sacramento, California, resident Zully Broussard. When a friend desperately needed a kidney, Zully, fifty years old, offered hers. However, during the screening process, surgeons located another kidney that was a better match. Zully was discharged with her organs intact and enough "friend cred" to last a lifetime. But she had come too far to turn back. She informed the hospital she wanted to go ahead and donate her kidney to another patient.

Zully's heroic decision inspired five others to donate their kidneys to strangers at the same hospital over the next forty-eight hours. The chain of kidney donations gave the gift of life to six patients.

When asked why she would endure the pain and take the risk of major surgery to help a stranger, Zully said she just felt compassion for people who have to endure the grind of dialysis treatments several times a week.[2] When issued a reprieve, most people would have raced from the hospital wiping perspiration from their brow and singing "Hallelujah." But Zully saw the big picture: several lives were saved because she fixed her eyes on what would be gained rather than on what would be lost.

Do you remember the last time you made a sacrifice to help someone in need? Maybe you gave away your favorite chair, mowed a neighbor's lawn, helped a classmate with homework, or stretched your budget to contribute to a charity. Chances are, afterward, you were either fulfilled or filled with regret. At times, sacrifice *can* hurt—but the pain doesn't have to last long. Take a cue from Zully: focus on the good that was accomplished. Through your kindness and sacrifice, you met another person's need and demonstrated that you're not simply living for yourself. You revealed that you have higher aspirations: for you, success is measured by what you give away—not by what you keep.

> *The value of a gift is measured by the kindness in your heart, not the wealth in your hand.*

Like Zully, you'll be presented with opportunities to sacrifice something you value for someone in need. It's not always an easy decision, but that's why sacrifice is such a loud expression of love. Here are two key questions to ask when deciding whether to make a sacrifice: Is it the right thing to do—will it truly meet a need? Can I give joyfully without regret? Your answers will lead you to a wise decision.

Imagine if you were broke and only had two cents to your name. Pretend for a moment that those two cents represent your only security, your last meal, and your only hope for a better day. Would you give them away? One woman did just that. Jesus put her radical sacrifice into context. He said, "The truth is that this poor widow gave more to the collection than all the others put together. All the others gave what they'll never miss; she gave extravagantly what she couldn't afford—she gave her all" (Mark 12:43–44).

Jesus wasn't disparaging the offerings of the rich. And he wasn't demanding equal sacrifice. Rather, he wanted to communicate two big ideas. First, what you give away—and what you hold on to—reveal a lot about what you value. Your level of sacrifice reflects the level of your commitment. Second, the value of a gift is measured by the kindness in your heart, not the wealth in your hand. Too often kindness and sacrifice are measured by the amount given, when the frequency and consistency of one's kindness are often more revealing.

Sacrifice often means denying what you want so others can receive what they need.

Everyday kindness is a strong indicator of one's love for and dedication to others. Your kind acts may go unnoticed by others, but God sees what you're doing. "Share what you have with others. God takes particular pleasure in acts of worship—a different kind of 'sacrifice'—that take place in kitchen and workplace and on the streets" (Heb. 13:16).

Radical sacrifice often means denying what you want so others can receive what they need. It may mean waiting to buy a new car until next year, wearing the same wardrobe for another few months, or reducing your premium coffee intake to four cups a week. The money saved can then be used to combat breast cancer, rescue abused animals, care for AIDS victims, provide school lunches to underprivileged kids, and much more. Radical sacrifice asks, "Should I have two of one thing when others have none?"

You might be asking, "I get helping friends and family members, but why should I make sacrifices for people I'll never meet?" That's a fair question, because sacrificial giving is not a contractual obligation. No one except you knows how much you give away. But ask yourself, can you really be happy knowing that others are suffering and you could have alleviated their pain with just a little sacrifice?

Their mission in life is to earn and gather more resources so they can give more away.

In his book *The Five People You Meet in Heaven*, author Mitch Albom says, "Sometimes when you sacrifice something precious, you're not really losing it. You're just passing it on to someone else."[3] Many have experienced the fulfillment that comes from "passing" their possessions to others. They've discovered more satisfaction from giving than receiving. Their mission in life is to earn and gather more resources so they can give more away. They see themselves as "channels of blessing" rather than "cisterns for storing." That's a lifestyle often summed up by the saying, "We make a living by what we get. We make a life by what we give."

Scientific studies suggest that humans are biologically created to care for one another. Psychologist Dacher Keltner says the vagus nerve—the nervous system's longest grouping of nerves—shows activity whenever people feel compassion. It fires when people see photographs of the poor and

42

suffering or hear stories of someone in distress. The nerve is also activated when people are inspired to make donations or sacrifices for someone in need. Keltner says, "The more you feel compassion, the stronger the Vagus nerve response." His study concluded that every person was "born to be good."[4]

Stefan Pressley, an eighteen-year-old high school senior, made the kind of sacrifice his teammates will never forget. After his brother gave him a 2002 Honda Civic, Stefan began saving toward the $500 he needed to get the car road ready. After months of working side jobs after school and on weekends, he achieved his goal. It was a surprise to his family, then, when he took the $500 and spent it on something completely different.

A member of the Pine Forest cross-country squad, Stefan knew the value of a well-made pair of running shoes. When he heard that some of his teammates couldn't afford decent shoes, he took the car money and purchased ten pairs of shoes—one for every member of his team. The dream of driving his own car to school his senior year would have to wait. When friends heard about his sacrifice, however, they created a web page for donations so Stefan could get his car fixed after all.

Troy Moon, reporter for the *Pensacola News Journal*, wrote about Stefan's sacrificial gift: "Part of me wants him to get that car fixed right away. But—and I hope this doesn't come off as cruel—part of me hopes it doesn't happen right away. Like I said, that's what makes a sacrifice a sacrifice. You do it, knowing that you are giving up something. That you will do without. If you get what you want, then what are you sacrificing? Again, I hope people understand what I'm saying here. But then again, maybe if he does get community assistance to get his car fixed . . . he'll learn that giving, sacrifice and compassion are contagious. That good deeds breed good deeds. That one person can make a difference."[5]

As Stefan demonstrated, people are more inclined to make sacrifices for their friends. It's an unwritten rule—they help you when others won't. They move your furniture up three flights of stairs, compliment your horrendous home-cooked meal, and loan you twenty dollars despite knowing you'll never pay it back. True friends don't keep score—they want to help. It's that same spirit that drives people like you to make sacrifices for complete strangers. Out of kindness and a sense of responsibility, you enlarge your circle of friends to include people you may never meet. You donate to victims of natural disasters and feed hungry children in developing nations, because they are your brothers and sisters too. It's at that level of kindness and sacrifice—when you tell yourself "no"—that you discover *less* is really *more*.

KIND WAYS

1. Sign up to become a blood or plasma donor.
2. Consider foster care or adoption. (In 2014, more than four hundred thousand children in the United States were not living with permanent families.[6])
3. Grow your hair long and donate your locks to organizations that make wigs for cancer patients.
4. Pay for a child to have cleft palate surgery in a developing country.
5. Encourage friends and family to donate to a charity of their choice, rather than giving you a present for your birthday.

CHAPTER FIVE

It's Not Expensive

I don't think you ever stop giving. I really don't. I think it's an
on-going process. And it's not just about being able to write
a check. It's being able to touch somebody's life.[1]

—Oprah Winfrey

National Guardsman Lt. Col. Frank Dailey was dining at a
Cracker Barrel restaurant when he received one of his highest
honors. The award came from eight-year-old Myles Eckert.
On his way into the restaurant, Myles found twenty dollars
in the parking lot. His initial thought was to buy a video
game, but then he spotted Dailey in uniform. Myles wrapped
the twenty dollars in a note that read, *"Dear Soldier, my dad
was a soldier. He's in heaven now. I found this $20 in the
parking lot when we got here. We like to pay it forward in
my family. It's your lucky day! Thank you for your service.
Myles Eckert—a gold star kid."*

Myles's father was killed in Iraq five weeks after Myles
was born. On his way home from the restaurant, Myles asked

his mother, Tiffany, to drive him by his father's grave. He wanted to spend some time alone with his dad. From a distance, Tiffany watched as Myles stared toward heaven and told his father details of his good deed.

Giving hope and encouragement to people is not expensive, but neither is it free.

He lingered quietly for a few moments as if waiting to hear his father say, "Job well done." Then with a smile and salute, the boy bid farewell.

That day Myles's act of kindness made his mother proud and left a lasting impression on Lt. Col. Dailey. The officer said he keeps the boy's note on his desk and reads it every morning as an inspiration to be generous too.[2]

Giving hope and encouragement to people is not expensive, but neither is it free. It requires you to choose a life of generosity so others can have a life of opportunity. Here are six principles to help guide your giving decisions:

1. *Generosity is sharing.* In the film *Cast Away*, Tom Hanks plays Chuck, a FedEx employee whose cargo plane crashes near a deserted island in the South Pacific. Chuck assumes he's been declared "lost at sea" and must fend for himself in a hostile environment. He's hungry and lonely but refuses to give up. He receives much-needed help when several FedEx packages filled with supplies wash ashore. Eventually, Chuck devises a plan and escapes the island.[3]

   Ask yourself, if you were marooned with other castaways on a remote island and had access to emergency supplies, would you share so others could live too? Well, you *do* live on an island—a global island called Earth with seven billion inhabitants,[4] where over eight hundred million people live in extreme poverty. One in five persons in developing regions live on less than $1.25 a day.[5] And nearly forty-seven million Americans live below the poverty line.[6] Someone's survival or happiness may depend on your willingness to share.

Kindness is not about taking a vow of poverty; it's about making a commitment to generosity. You don't need to go sell your favorite video games, jewelry, or car. You don't need to stop shopping at Macy's or grabbing pizza at Domino's.

> *You live on . . . a global island called Earth with seven billion inhabitants, where over eight hundred million people live in extreme poverty.*

Rather, when opportunities present themselves, simply be willing to share what you have with people who don't.

2. *Generosity requires making room.* Perhaps you live one paycheck to the next. You don't have a lot of extra money lying around to give away. Well, you're not alone. Before many can give, they have to create financial breathing room by making adjustments to their spending habits. That is a difficult step for some to take—and not because they struggle with greed. Rather, they wrestle with the fear of going without.

In recent years, even though the average family size decreased, the square footage of homes rose significantly.[7] At the same time, there was a 50 percent increase in rented storage space.[8] Today, 10 percent of the households in the United States rent a storage unit.[9] All of this suggests one thing: Americans have more stuff than they know what to do with. Perhaps it's a good time for a yard sale!

3. *Generosity maintains a meaningful existence.* If you want to really live, then learn to generously give. Choose to be openhanded rather than tightfisted. Find as much pleasure giving presents as you do unwrapping them. The adrenaline rush that comes from owning something new doesn't compare to the fulfillment of knowing you made someone happy.

   If you're discouraged or licking your wounds from a disappointment, change your outlook by moving beyond how you feel and focusing on how others feel. Take your eyes off your needs and fix your attention on meeting the needs of others. By helping them, you help yourself.

4. *Generosity multiplies itself.* Just a little generosity can reproduce a lot of kindness. Every time you demonstrate compassion, you are a billboard for kindness. You inspire others to follow your example. When you say a kind word, others are more inclined to say a kind word. When you give to someone in need, others tend to reach into their wallets and make a donation too. Your acts of kindness are often emulated, and they accomplish collectively what you can't do alone.

5. *Generosity requires responsibility.* You can't give to everyone, but you can give to someone. So, make your giving count. When making donations, ensure that the charity is reputable. Find out what percentage of your donation will actually go to addressing the need. If the recipient is an individual, ask for verification of how the

funds were spent. Don't allow your generosity to be exploited and your good intentions to be thwarted. There are too many people who really need your help.

Don't allow your generosity to be exploited and your good intentions to be thwarted.

6. *Generosity is impulsive.* Sometimes compassion demands an immediate decision: You see a homeless family on the side of the road. A senior citizen's utilities are turned off. A college student faces dismissal because he or she is short on tuition. An African village needs a well so families can have clean drinking water. In some cases, there isn't time for due diligence. You simply have to follow your heart and err on the side of "impulsive generosity." Live by the adage, "Seldom resist the impulse to do something kind."

Waitress Kayla Lane followed *her* heart when she learned that patrons Shaun and Debbie Riddle had recently lost their nine-week-old baby. Impulsively, she decided to pay for their meal. Instead of receiving a bill, the couple found a note that read, "Your ticket has been paid for. We are terribly sorry for your loss. God Bless—West Side Café."

Kayla told the couple the restaurant had taken care of the bill *and* her tip. But the manager later confirmed that Kayla had paid for it personally. She had earned a reputation among her coworkers for paying for the meals of soldiers, police officers, and firefighters.

"I didn't want any recognition," she said. "I just wanted the satisfaction of being a helping hand in a time of sorrow for this family."[10]

A pilot for Frontier Airlines also earned a spot in the "impulsive generosity" hall of fame when his plane was forced to land in Cheyenne, Wyoming. Extreme weather had diverted the flight from Denver. But his 157 hungry passengers were required to remain aboard for several hours as the plane rested on the tarmac awaiting instructions. Fortunately, the pilot knew what to do. Thinking quickly, he called Domino's and ordered thirty pizzas. Within forty-five minutes the pizzas were delivered to a plane filled with cheering passengers. The pilot paid for the food personally and left a handsome tip for the delivery guy too.[11] That's the definition of generosity.

Early Jewish tradition required farmers to leave the corners of their fields untouched and unharvested so the poor and suffering could wander in and find something to eat. Farmers believed God would provide a plentiful harvest if they simply followed his instructions. Today, you have a harvest consisting of time, talent, and resources. Whether you believe in God or not, there is something noble and profound about setting aside a portion of your fields to help others. And when you do, don't be surprised if you too experience a more plentiful harvest.

KIND WAYS

1. Take part in feedONE* or other nonprofit campaigns that feed impoverished children.
2. Pay the tab for the customer sitting behind you in the drive-through line.

*feedONE (feedone.org) is a campaign that encourages individuals to feed one child each year for $10 per month.

3. Assist your children with going through their toys and donating the ones they no longer want.

4. Raise donations from coworkers for an employee benevolence fund.

5. Leave a stack of quarters at a Laundromat.

CHAPTER SIX

Stop the Clock!

The best expression of love is time. The best time to love is now.[1]

—Rick Warren

Dustin and Sarah and their three sons were enjoying a sunny day at their favorite swimming hole near Maine's Mt. Katahdin. Dustin, who served in the military, was being deployed overseas for many months, so this was a day to cherish being together as a family. Unfortunately, the fun ended abruptly when Dustin's wedding band slipped off his finger and was lost in the rushing rapids of the Penobscot River.

Sarah cried on her husband's shoulder that afternoon. The ring symbolized eleven years of marriage—every scratch a monument to the joy and pain they'd experienced together.

Dustin wiped away her tears, saying, "Honey, don't worry—we'll buy a new ring."

Weeks passed. Dustin was deployed. And Sarah and the boys were alone. They had given up hope of ever finding the ring.

When the *Bangor Daily* newspaper picked up the story of the lost ring, Sarah received numerous emails from sympathetic readers. One message in particular caught her attention. A man named Zack wrote: "Could you please give me a call as my father and I have found a wedding band and would like you to identify it?"

The following day, a cautious Sarah met Zack and Greg in a parking lot outside a restaurant. The men explained that the newspaper article had inspired them to spend an entire day searching for her ring. Greg was a professional diver and knew the area fairly well. He reached into his pocket and retrieved a plastic bag containing a ring.

> *Perhaps as a full-time student, employee, or parent, you already feel overloaded with obligations.*

Sarah nodded emphatically, tears surfacing in her eyes. Her hand trembled as Greg placed the ring in her palm. Though they were complete strangers, she threw her arms around the men. Their act of kindness—and investment of time—had reunited her with much more than a ring. They had reunited her with memories more precious than diamonds.[2]

Time is arguably your most valuable commodity. Unlike gold or diamonds, time cannot be bought, borrowed, hoarded, or earned. As the seconds tick away, your time is yours to use as you choose. But, like many, you may feel you don't have the extra time to stop and show someone kindness. Perhaps as a full-time student, employee, or parent, you already feel overloaded with obligations. How do you find a little time to invest in others? Here are three steps you can take to create margin in your life for both planned and spontaneous acts of kindness.

First, experiment with keeping a time log for one week, recording how you spend your time each day. You might be surprised how much discretionary time is dedicated to leisure activities and entertainment. One study revealed that 79 percent of Americans watch television or participate in some form of social media at least 3.5 hours per day.[3]

Planning is imperative, but sometimes kindness requires spontaneity.

Second, ask yourself, if you had more discretionary time, what are some of the things you would do for others? Write out your wish list.

And, third, establish new habits and discipline by setting aside one hour each week for serving others: volunteer at your child's school or a local animal shelter, make phone calls for a civic organization, raise money for a charity, offer to represent your pastor by visiting members in the hospital or nursing home. Start small and build from there.

Planning is imperative, but sometimes kindness requires spontaneity. Don't miss an opportunity to be kind because your "kindness hours" are 8:00–10:00 a.m. on the second Tuesday of every month. Take a moment each day—no matter how brief or inconvenient—to stop and brighten someone's day. Your gift of time could make all the difference. As author Dr. Leo Buscaglia said, "Too often we underestimate the power of a touch, a smile, a kind word, a listening ear, an honest compliment, or the smallest act of caring, all of which have the potential to turn a life around."[4]

One afternoon actor Mark Hamill decided to break out of the Hollywood bubble and take control of his calendar. He skipped a promotional appearance for the movie *The Force Awakens* so he could help some kids. Mark, who plays Luke Skywalker, drove to a local hospital to visit sick children. When a newspaper reporter inquired about his decision, Mark replied, "*Star Wars* movies are meant to be a couple of hours of diversion from reality, and we need that. They are optimistic and hopeful stories." But, he added, such things are "very trivial" compared to bringing comfort to ailing kids.[5]

Are you living in a bubble of obligation? When you look at your calendar, do you feel trapped? Perhaps, like Mark, you need to break out of your routine and invest a little time in helping some children. Consider coaching a Little League team, leading a Scout troop, volunteering as a Big Brother or Big Sister, or teaching youth at your church. Only you can make the adjustments necessary to substitute "trivial" pursuits with meaningful ones. The remote is in your hands; it's up to you to find more time to do something kind.

KIND WAYS

1. Ring a bell for the Salvation Army during the holidays.
2. Offer to babysit a young couple's children so they can have a date night.
3. Assist a graduate with their résumé and with locating a job.
4. Grocery shop for someone who is disabled.
5. Take two friends who are elderly to the park so they can enjoy the fresh air and sunshine together.

CHAPTER SEVEN

The Power of "With"

It's often just enough to be with someone. I don't need to
touch them. Not even talk. A feeling passes between you both.
You're not alone.[1]

—Marilyn Monroe

Neither teenager asked for pity or special treatment. Leroy
Sutton had lost his legs in a freight train accident, and Dartanyon Crockett had been declared legally blind due to a
degenerative disease. Each just needed a friend. Fortunately
they found what they were looking for in each other. Their
respective challenges had brought the two high school wres-
tlers together and made them inseparable.

The pair could be spotted in the high school hallways, at
wrestling matches, and at the mall. Dartanyon carried his
170-pound friend everywhere on his back. He provided the
horsepower—Leroy provided the navigation.

Together they were a force on the wrestling mat too, representing Lincoln-West High in Cleveland, Ohio. Dartanyon

captured the league title, and Leroy won nine matches. At each contest, they could be seen cheering each other to victory. Dartanyon said, "We pushed each other to our limits, and we didn't let each other give up."

When it came time to graduate, Leroy didn't have to ride Dartanyon's back across the stage to receive his diploma. Instead, with newly fitted prosthetic legs, he and Dartanyon walked across the stage together. "It meant so much to me," said Leroy, "to know I had a friend who was there to catch me if I stumbled."[2]

Leroy and Dartanyon discovered the value of the four-letter word "with." They accomplished more together than they did apart. Likewise you have the power to help others reach new heights by simply walking *with* them. Your presence and involvement in their lives are an act of kindness that is often underestimated. Think about the selfless people who made themselves available when *you* needed a friend. Chances are it was not their words or a particular gift that evoked gratitude; rather, it was their willingness to walk alongside you.

Every person is born with a need for companionship. That's why loneliness sets in so quickly. Some crimes and social problems can be traced back to a lack of intimacy. How different the world would be if everyone had a friend. When you see people who are alone, do you have compassion for them? The Latin root of the word *compassion* means "to suffer with."

A seventy-year-old woman demonstrated the power of "suffering with" on a sky train in Vancouver, British Columbia. A man suddenly became aggressive: cursing, shouting, and frightening the other passengers. Bravely the woman smiled and extended her hand. She held it at the man's chest for a few seconds until he finally obliged. Instantly he calmed down and trouble was averted. The two held hands for twenty minutes until the man arrived at his destination. After he exited the train, another passenger congratulated the peacemaker: "God bless you—the world needs more people like you." When asked why she held his hand, she said, "I didn't want him to feel so alone. I'm a mother. I have two sons around his age, and life puts you in hard places sometimes."[3]

Sometimes there is no substitute for turning off your cell phone and giving someone your full attention.

Each day offers an array of "with" opportunities: playing a video game with your children, sitting with a senior citizen, having lunch with a classmate or coworker, power walking with a neighbor, or just hanging out with a friend at Starbucks. Sometimes there is no substitute for turning off your cell phone and giving someone your full attention.

One day a young girl tiptoed toward her father, who was camped in a recliner reading a magazine. The television was providing background noise. "Daddy," she exclaimed, "something great happened to me today." Without looking up, he said, "Tell me about it." Determined to get his attention, she pleaded, "Daddy, it's important—can you at least listen to me with your eyes?"

Being "with" people is becoming more challenging with the advent of social media. Although Facebook, Snapchat, and Twitter, for example, provide a platform for enlarging one's circle of friends, they also threaten to replace the need for intimacy.

In other words, people are becoming more comfortable being alone.

One study revealed that college students have 40 percent less empathy than their counterparts of twenty years ago.[4] It cites social networking as a significant reason. Sean Parker, cofounder of Facebook and creator of Napster, described relational detachment as a possible result of social media: "We talk internally [about] restoring intimacy in a world where social [media] has connected us to more people than ever and yet somehow we feel more lonely as a result of it—or at least I do. It's maybe one of the unintended consequences of having a billion people on social media and having 300 or more, on average, friends or followers. . . . There is a certain loneliness that comes from having so many fast superficial interactions with so many people."[5]

> *One study revealed that college students have 40 percent less empathy than their counterparts of twenty years ago.*

Social media has brought enormous value to society. But kindness and compassion are difficult to express from behind a computer screen or from a distance. Consequently, you may need to apply the *"oikos* strategy" to your life. (And no, that's not referring to the brand of yogurt.) *Oikos* is a Greek word referring to four types of relationships: family, friends, acquaintances, and strangers. Make it your goal to show kindness to—and be with—at least one person in each *oikos* category every week. Before long, the practice will become a permanent way of life.

There are a million excuses for not spending time with people. Perhaps you've used a few. You've told yourself, *I've worked all day and I just need to chill out; I have to focus on my own problems right now*; *I want to watch television and eat ice cream*; or, *I'm tired of talking and listening to people—I'll send them an email.* There's no need to feel guilty for having those thoughts and emotions. It doesn't mean you're selfish or unkind. Everyone needs space. Life is fast paced and down time helps you cope and find perspective. But, if you're not careful, occasional retreats

> *There are a million excuses for not spending time with people.*

can become a comfortable pattern. And, without realizing it, meaningful relationships can suffer, because you're not investing in one another.

Maroon 5 lead singer Adam Levine illustrated the power of "with" when meeting one of his fans. Christopher Warner, a ten-year-old with Down syndrome, caught Adam's attention after posting a video message. Adam invited the boy and his friends to a live performance in Washington, DC. But backstage at the concert, an awestruck Christopher suffered a panic attack and crouched to the floor. Reading the situation, Adam and his band lay quietly beside the boy and settled his nerves. Before long, Christopher was back on his feet exchanging hugs and slapping high fives with Adam and the band. That night, from the front row, Levine's "number one fan" enjoyed the concert of a lifetime.[6]

It would have been easier for Adam to rush on stage that night and let someone else care for Christopher. But his willingness to stay with the boy remedied the situation and brought a lasting smile to a ten-year-old's face. *Your* willingness to spend time with others seals your relationships and assures friends that they do not face their challenges alone.

61

In 1979 Mother Teresa was awarded the Nobel Peace Prize. During a banquet to honor her lifetime achievement, she appeared wearing a simple Indian sari—attire more suited for a peasant than a prizewinner. The guests stood to their feet and applauded as she shuffled to the podium. With a gentle and feeble voice, she addressed the crowd: "Find the poor here, right in your own home, first, and then begin to love there, and find out about your next-door neighbor." She paused before asking, "Do you even know who your neighbors are?"[7]

That night Mother Teresa reminded the audience that kindness begins with knowing your neighbor by name. But it doesn't end there. Kindness requires that you look people in the eye and dignify them with a smile. It often requires a touch, a helping hand, a thoughtful word, or just being "with."

KIND WAYS

1. Develop a calendar of special events that you will attend with family members and friends.
2. Volunteer to be a reading buddy at an elementary school.
3. Deliver flowers to residents in a senior citizens home. If you play a musical instrument—bring that too!
4. Arrange for hot meals to be provided for a family who has lost a loved one.
5. Shake the hands of veterans and thank them for their service.

CHAPTER EIGHT

Take a Breath

When you have good friends you've been around, every time they talk, you don't give them your full attention. You don't look them in the eye and stop. Half the time, you're listening, half the time, you are ignoring them. [1]

—Matthew McConaughey

Listening is kindness.

It tells people you cherish their words and value their opinion. It says, "You matter."

Nasir Sobhani is not your typical barber. Tattoos cover swaths of his body. He rides a skateboard and openly acknowledges that he was once a drug addict. Once a week, he can be found skating around Melbourne, Australia, carrying a case of styling tools under his arm. He's looking for homeless people who need a professional haircut or shave.

While cutting their hair, "The Street Barber" seizes the opportunity to engage in friendly dialogue. Most people, he says, really want conversation and companionship. He asks

YOUR NEXT 24 HOURS

tough questions and naturally laces each chat with kindness, optimism, and words of encouragement. "So what if a person smells or a person's on drugs or was on drugs?" he says. "At the end of the day, they're all people that we should love."

Nasir recounts many of his conversations on his blog. He wrote about a single mom named Rachael, twenty-eight, who has lived on the streets since she was thirteen. She ran away from her negligent parents and became addicted to heroin. "I was so shocked and saddened when I heard that. I couldn't say anything for a bit and had to cut her hair in silence. She said it was her first [real] haircut since she left home. When she saw what she looked like she couldn't believe it was her."[2]

> *Listening gives friendship a chance. Without it, one person is the narrator and the other is just the audience.*

The Street Barber has earned a reputation for cutting hair, but he's also made a lot of new friends because he takes the time to learn their names and listen to their stories. He's demonstrated that kindness means seeing the unseen, hearing the unheard, and touching the unloved.

Sometimes all it takes to send a message that you care is a simple nod, a sincere smile, a single tear, or just hearing people out. Every time you listen to their stories and hear the echoes of their lives, you spread a little kindness.

Listening gives friendship a chance. Without it, one person is the narrator and the other is just the audience. Dr. Ralph Nichols, a listening legend, said, "The most basic of all human needs is the need to understand and be understood. The best way to understand people is to listen to them."[3] The Bible also encourages listening: "Understand this, my dear brothers and sisters: You must all be quick to listen, slow to speak, and slow to get angry" (James 1:19 NLT).

Talking and listening at the same time is nearly impossible. And, in most instances, people are more inclined to listen if you make your words *count*—and less inclined if you let your words *mount*. People prefer humble and sincere dialogue to high and mighty monologues. Meaningful conversations build relationships while condescending lectures bulldoze them.

People prefer humble and sincere dialogue to high and mighty monologues.

Remember, not every conversation needs to be about you. Instead of "parking" on your achievements or dropping names, learn to deflect attention and shift conversations back to others. Rather than wasting time chasing accolades, focus on pursuing deeper relationships. You'll likely have more friends if you're a good listener too, because people won't run and hide every time they see you coming.

It's difficult to monopolize a conversation and, at the same time, benefit from one. Here are some simple ways to determine whether you're a talker rather than a listener:

1. Do you speak in long, protracted sentences without taking a breath?
2. Do you share your lunch plans, dinner menu, and weight-loss strategies before asking how the listener is doing?
3. While talking on the phone, can friends lay their phone down to go use the restroom and return without you knowing they left?
4. Do you repeatedly finish other people's sentences?

5. Can you hold a phone in each hand and carry on two separate conversations at the same time?

There is a time to talk and a time to listen. Conversation demonstrates mutual respect. And, with respect comes cooperation and collaboration. Discoveries are made—and lives are changed—when people take time to listen to one another. How many contestants on television's *The Voice* have been launched into lucrative recording careers because someone listened to their music? How many cures for diseases have been discovered because someone listened to a new theory? How many malnourished children have been rescued because someone heard a cry for help? The world is a fairer place—a kinder place—when people like you listen.

*Listening also means hearing what people are **not** saying.*

Listening also means hearing what people are *not* saying. Some are wounded, alone, and afraid. Their jobs may be tenuous and their family fractured, and you'd never know it. They suffer in silence because they really don't know whom they can trust. It will take someone like you, who hears what's *not* being said, to reach out to them and offer encouragement.

Toronto Blue Jays third baseman Josh Donaldson had to overcome a troubled childhood before being voted Major League Baseball's Most Valuable Player. He credits conversations with his high school coach, Lloyd Skoda, for helping him turn his life around.

As an only child, Josh saw his parents divorce before he reached grade school. His father was later sentenced to prison on drug charges. His mother, Lisa, wanting to make sure

Josh was surrounded by the right influences, enrolled him in Faith Academy, a private Catholic high school in Mobile, Alabama. Coach Skoda soon became the boy's father figure.

Skoda told the *Globe and Mail*, "Me and Josh would sit around and talk, and it wasn't just about baseball stuff. We'd talk about life stuff. He was fun to coach, a great guy, but he had some issues with his personality. He wasn't really abrasive, but if [he] got his feelings hurt a little bit he was always ready to fight. He was a tough kid, but a good kid at the same time."[4]

Josh confided to his coach that he felt like he didn't have any friends on the team, and it was his own fault. Skoda recruited the help of a few players, and together they took Josh under their wing. By the time he graduated, he had matured into a valued member of the team. Josh was awarded a baseball scholarship to Auburn University, before being drafted by the Chicago Cubs. But much of his success can be traced back to a coach who invested his time in listening to a boy who just needed a friend.

If you have a penchant for monopolizing conversations, take a deep breath, count to ten, and decide today to become a better listener. When you do, people will see that you value their words as much as your own.

KIND WAYS

1. Put away your cell phone when in a group conversation.
2. When someone else is talking, keep eye contact and don't interrupt.

3. Make an effort to remember the names of the people you meet.

4. While sitting in the chair, ask your barber or hairstylist to tell you his or her story.

5. Seek the advice of others when making an important decision.

CHAPTER NINE

Speak and Destroy?

For beautiful eyes, look for the good in others; for beautiful
lips, speak only words of kindness; and for poise, walk with
the knowledge that you are never alone.[1]

—Audrey Hepburn

What difference can one handwritten letter make? Well, an
anonymous writer in London, England, believes words have
the power to give hope and joy to unsuspecting strangers. She
has left hundreds of encouraging letters all over London: on
train seats, pinned to bulletin boards, stuffed in magazine
racks, and more.

Revealing her motivation, the writer said, "I hope to bring
some warmth, comfort and encouragement to people. And
when I read them back to myself, I often find that I've writ-
ten something I actually needed to hear myself. But that's
how it is with unconditional giving: you always get back so
much more than you give."[2]

Words have such power.

Consider whether the words you give to others are bayonets or bouquets. "Words kill, words give life; they're either poison or fruit—you choose" (Prov. 18:21). Your words—along with your tone—have the power to victimize or liberate. They can suppress people's happiness for decades or inspire joy for a lifetime. An Oxford University study showed that many who suffer from depression as adults were wounded by harsh and demeaning words as children.[3]

Your words are the mortar that binds your family and friendships together. Studies confirm that people are more likely to respond to kind and considerate words than they are to animosity and arm-twisting. When you're attacked, it's human nature to return fire with fire. But a gentle reply often makes a stronger impression. Mother Teresa said, "Kind words can be short and easy to speak, but their echoes are truly endless."[4]

If you have children or a spouse, you may be tempted to resort to name calling or harsh demands to get their attention and alter their behavior. But rest assured, your words will be remembered when all the smoke clears. One sentence spoken in anger or haste can be completely forgotten by the speaker and, years later, be quoted verbatim by the recipient. Use wisdom in the heat of battle and measure your words carefully. And if you've crossed the line and said things you regret, don't be afraid to ask for forgiveness.

When you're attacked, it's human nature to return fire with fire. But a gentle reply often makes a stronger impression.

Take a moment to consider the issues that trigger conflict and disagreement in your life: work, school, finances, schedules, parenting, in-laws, and more. Ask yourself whether you can take a kinder approach that would result in fewer arguments, less stress, and more cooperation.

Look for opportunities to deposit words of kindness to family members, friends, and total strangers: compliment someone's clothes, write a note of appreciation, or congratulate a co-worker for a job well done. One kind word, spoken with sincerity, can make a person's day. One thank-you note can transform a scowl into a smile.

One sentence spoken in anger or haste can be completely forgotten by the speaker and, years later, be quoted verbatim by the recipient.

Restaurant owner Ashley Jiron decided to put her kindness in writing. One afternoon she noticed that someone—in search of a meal—had rummaged through her dumpster behind P.B. Jams restaurant in Warr Acres, Oklahoma. Ashley decided that was unacceptable. But she didn't get angry, call the police, or put a padlock on the dumpster. Instead, she posted signs around her building with the following message: *To the person going through our trash for their next meal: You're a human being and worth more than a meal from a dumpster. Please come in during operating hours for a classic PB&J, fresh veggies, and a cup of water at no charge. No questions asked. Your friend—The Owner.*

"We've all been in that position where we needed somebody's help," Ashley told KFOR, "and we just needed somebody to extend a hand." The experience led Ashley to start a campaign called "Share the Nuts."[5] Customers at the restaurant now have the opportunity to prepay for a

YOUR NEXT 24 HOURS

meal for someone in need and to leave the recipient a note of encouragement.

Don't underestimate the power of words spoken in love and kindness. When you deliver encouragement to people who are hurting, you help them believe tomorrow can be better than today. To a troubled soul, your words are more comforting than an eloquent speech. You may not know the story of their struggle or the circumstances that turned their world upside down. That doesn't matter. Just don't hold back because you fear failure or rejection. Your words could be all a person needs to break free from the past and regain hope. If you're led by kindness, you possess the words to restore a homeless man's dignity, inspire a child to believe in herself, lift the spirits of a single mother, help a youth overcome shame and disappointment, and salute a senior citizen for a life well lived. The kindness inside you has the power to transform lives.

The kindness inside you has the power to transform lives.

Schoolchildren in Arlington, Washington, used two unforgettable words to express their appreciation to ninety-three-year-old Louise Edlen.[6] For five years, Louise faithfully waved at the children as their bus passed her living room window on the way to school. She became known as "the grandma in the window."

But one September morning, she wasn't in the window. Days passed and still no sign of "Grandma." Everyone was worried. Finally, bus driver Carol Mitzelfeldt stopped by Louise's home. There was no answer at the door, so she left a bouquet of flowers with a note that read, *To the Grandma in the window. We're thinking of you. Love—the kids on Bus 7 and bus driver, Carol.*

The following day, Carol was contacted by Louise's husband. He informed her that Louise had suffered a stroke and was receiving treatment at a rehabilitation center. When the students heard about Grandma's condition, they decided to do something to cheer her up. They enlarged a group photograph of them waving out the windows of Bus 7 and had each student sign it.

Carol had the honor of personally delivering the photograph to Louise at the center. Although it was difficult for her to speak, she managed to smile with her eyes and whisper to Carol that the children meant a lot to her.

Weeks later, when Grandma finally returned home, she could once again be seen sitting in the window. And the kids of Bus 7 were ready for her. As the bus passed, she noticed the large sign hanging in the bus window. It read, "Welcome Home."

The world could use more signs—positive signs. At times, it feels like negativity and slander are on repeat. In the media and real life, conflict has become a form of entertainment. But, have you noticed that no one walks away satisfied? When you're with people who prefer to gossip and complain, don't join in the pessimism . . . because you may be their only source for optimism. Instead, fill your vocabulary with words that are uplifting and hopeful, and let them see there's still a lot of good in the world.

KIND WAYS

1. Say "Thank you!" "Please," and "You're welcome" as often as you can.

2. Praise a courteous and efficient service provider to his or her supervisor.

3. Compliment someone every day for his or her appearance, character, or positive attitude.

4. Give up complaining for a week and decide to be more positive, optimistic, and affirming of others.

5. Stop and talk to a homeless person holding a sign on a street corner.

CHAPTER TEN

Welcome to Reality TV

Most things are good, and they are the strongest things; but there are evil things too. . . . The important thing is to teach a child that good can always triumph over evil.[1]

—Walt Disney

Lee Beck, thirty-two, and his daughter, Amelie, seven, decided to celebrate their May birthdays differently than most do. Rather than wear party hats, blow out candles, and open presents, they performed thirty-nine acts of kindness to represent their combined ages. "I thought we could make this year special by doing something together," Lee said.

Their first act of kindness was to leave money at an amusement park ride so kids could ride for free. Their next act was to give schoolteachers boxes of chocolates. From there the deeds included making donations to the homeless, picking up trash in a park, leaving pennies at a wishing well, writing letters of gratitude to friends, providing a gift card for a family in need, and Lee registering as an organ donor.

According to Lee and Amelie, this is how they plan to celebrate their respective birthdays every year. "Next year it will be 41 acts of kindness," he said.[2]

"Start children off on the way they should go, and even when they are old they will not turn from it" (Prov. 22:6 NIV). Amelie's parents have certainly taught her valuable lessons in kindness and living a good life. At a young age, she's learned that serving others leads to greater fulfillment and happiness than simply serving yourself.

Author Rose Kennedy, mother of President John F. Kennedy, said, "When you hold your baby in your arms the first time and you think of all the things you can say and do to influence him, it's a tremendous responsibility. What you do with him can influence not only him, but everyone he meets and not for a day or a month or a year but for time and eternity."[3]

If you're a parent, you are the executive producer in a reality TV show called *Home*. Your children watch and learn every day. If they observe conflict and disrespect—that's what they'll emulate. If they see love and mutual respect—that too will guide their lives. How your family members interact with one another determines whether the reality show is a drama, comedy, or action adventure: Do you forgive one another? Do you disagree in private? Do you remain optimistic? Do you display affection? Do you laugh together? These are all factors in creating a healthy atmosphere in the home.

Parental inconsistency can be disturbing to children. If they see their parents having one persona at home and another in public, it evokes questions of authenticity. And if they hear their parents criticizing others or raising their voices at one another, it only adds to their confusion.

Remember, there's coming a time when your children will resolve their problems the same way you do.

If your parents did not provide you with the best example, determine not to use *their* failures to excuse your own. If nothing else, take note of their shortcomings and determine that you'll do better with your children. There's a lot riding on what happens in homes like yours. If enough families are built on a foundation of kindness, communities will see crime rates fall, domestic disputes decline, suicides drop, teenage pregnancies wane, and cases of child abuse fade.

Each home is a unique environment, presenting its own mix of battleground and beachfront. But the culture in your home frequently transfers from one generation to the next. The harmony you foster—and the hostility you allow—today could be your legacy for decades. But you can nurture kindness in your home in a myriad of ways: finish household chores, listen when someone's had a difficult day, be on time for family gatherings, hug one another and say "I love you," celebrate one another's victories, attend each other's special events, share the TV remote or family computer, and more. One of the best ways to express love to your children and build security in the home is to show love to your spouse.

> *Each home is a unique environment, presenting its own mix of battleground and beachfront.*

The home environment is not just a reflection of what you say and do; it's also influenced by your entertainment choices. Carefully select the programs that appear on your family's television or computer screen. Guard children from shows that are gratuitously violent or sexually explicit. The rude way in which journalists and politicians speak to one another on television can also have a negative effect. Take a few moments to help your children understand the difference between passionate discourse and personal attacks.

Children who are shown love are more likely to show love. That proved to be the case for seven-year-old Ryan Scroggin. She had endured eight surgeries for a rare bone and joint condition, but all she could think about was doing something to help the other children in the University of Oklahoma hospital.

Ryan was deeply affected by the death of a two-year-old boy in the bed next to hers during one of her hospital stays. This was the catalyst for her wish. "I don't want any presents for my birthday," she said to her parents. "I don't want a party. I want to go to the hospital and give stuffed animals to kids that are really sick."

She wrote a personal letter requesting stuffed animals that was posted on Facebook and in the window of a thrift store in Norman, Oklahoma. It didn't take long before stuffed animals started pouring in. One woman donated five hundred. Several weeks later, sixty Jeeps from a dealership in Oklahoma City delivered hundreds of stuffed animals to the hospital.

Ryan's grandmother told *Today*, "Ryan can't play with a whole lot of stuff because of her disabilities, but she's satisfied. She never asks for more. She just wants other people to have stuff." The family has since made the stuffed animal drive an annual event, benefitting children in a different city each year.[4]

The Scroggin and Beck families strengthened their respective homes by promoting kindness and selflessness among their children. You can encourage a spirit of giving in your family too. No home is perfect; every family faces its share of ups and downs. But a home founded on love and kindness can weather any storm. When crises arise, you can stand with confidence and say, "We are family and, no matter what, we're going to make it through these challenges together."

KIND WAYS

1. Stay connected to family members through video calls.
2. Volunteer to be a playground monitor at your children's school.
3. Excuse your child from class one afternoon and do something fun together.
4. Place notes of encouragement in the lunch of your child or significant other.
5. Cook a meal as a family and give it away to your neighbor.

CHAPTER ELEVEN

Remove the Handcuffs

Resentment is like drinking poison and then hoping it will kill your enemies.[1]

—Nelson Mandela

Anaheim Angels slugger Albert Pujols stepped into the pitch and blasted the ball high and toward the center field wall. All Tampa Bay Rays reliever Andrew Bellati could do was watch it sail over the fence for Albert's second home run of the night.

Giving up a home run is never a positive outcome for a pitcher. But for Andrew, a bad night in the big leagues was far better than a good night in jail. In 2010, when he was just nineteen, the big leaguer was sentenced for unintentionally killing a man while speeding on a rain-slicked road in Southern California.

Andrew could have served seven years in prison for manslaughter if not for an extraordinary act of mercy by the victim's wife, Lynette Reid. She had received a handwritten letter from Andrew, detailing his deep regret and error in judgment. He asked for her forgiveness.

During the trial—despite the fact Andrew had left her children fatherless—Lynette pleaded for leniency. "I think Andrew has owned up to it and tried to come out the other side a better man. I just couldn't see where him going to prison would help me or my children or anything else." Besides, she said she knew that's what her husband would have wanted.

Because of Lynette's appeal for mercy, Andrew spent less than 90 days in jail before resuming his baseball career. Now every time he marches to the pitcher's mound, Andrew says he is thankful for the opportunity he's been given.[2] He's living out his childhood dream because a widow and her children gave him a second chance.

You can either remain bitter or find a way to forgive and put an end to the tyranny of the past.

Perhaps you have been betrayed, slandered, demoted, neglected, or abused. You are not alone. At one time or another, everyone experiences a degree of injustice. Unfortunately, the agony and emotional scars can linger for years. You may never forget what happened, but you can find a way to press on with peace and perspective. You can either remain bitter or find a way to forgive and put an end to the tyranny of the past. Recovery may not happen overnight, but you can begin the healing process with one decision.

When my father was hit and killed by a drunken driver, I wrestled with a host of emotions. I bounced between a desire for revenge and feelings of self-pity. Everything from the holes in my shoes to the limp in my mother's walk reminded me of the injustice. At first, it was difficult to find sympathy for the driver. After all, he walked away without a scratch and, after a few months, strode out of jail ready to resume a normal life. We were the ones sentenced to a life of empty cupboards and hand-me-downs. As far as I was concerned, there was nothing fair or just about it. How could I ever forget what had happened?

But, in my pain, I was faced with a choice: I could allow myself to be ruled by bitterness and self-pity, or I could pardon the driver and not allow the accident to plague me for decades. I chose to forgive and so can you. I found peace and perspective and so can you.

Forgiveness is an act of kindness to perpetrators who may or may not deserve to be pardoned. Some may be oblivious—unaware that they have even hurt you. Others may know exactly what they've done but see little value in your forgiveness. Regardless of their attitude, you can choose to forgive in order to liberate yourself from their clutches. You can remove the handcuffs that have imprisoned you for far too long—because the pain of forgiving is far less than the pain of not forgiving. As Bishop T. D. Jakes said, "I think the first step is to understand that forgiveness does not exonerate the perpetrator. Forgiveness liberates the victim. It's a gift you give yourself."[3]

Unforgiveness has been found to also cause health problems. It increases blood pressure, affects cholesterol levels, and decreases blood flow through the coronary arteries. In addition, bitterness has been associated with creating problems in the immune system, causing chronic pain, and even contributing to cancer.[4] If you've struggled to forgive yourself, don't allow guilt to take a toll on your health and relationships. Instead, ask others to forgive you, attempt to pay restitution, and then rest your head on your pillow knowing you've done all you can to make things right. It's time to press on, because the opportunities before you are far more important than the regrets behind you.

When you demonstrate a willingness to forgive, others are more likely to forgive you. And your example may inspire them to forgive family members, employers, classmates, and neighbors who have caused them pain. They too will discover the happiness and freedom that comes from maintaining an attitude of forgiveness. Martin Luther King Jr. said, "Forgiveness is not an occasional act, it is a constant attitude."[5]

How different the world would be if more people made a practice of saying "I'm sorry" and "I forgive you"—and actually meant it.

Every day offers new opportunities to forgive: the waiter serves you decaffeinated coffee instead of regular, a motorist hijacks your parking space, your neighbor's dog barks and growls incessantly, your houseguest leaves a mess in the bathroom, your teenager lies to you about missing curfew. The list is endless. Each day you choose whether to retaliate in anger, fret in silence, or forgive and press on. For their sake—and yours—open your arms and say, "All is forgiven."

Rather than summon the police, actor Johnny Depp, star of *Pirates of the Caribbean*, chose to forgive a man who accosted him and singer Stephen Jones of the band Babybird. Brandishing a broken bottle outside a Los Angeles recording studio, the mugger demanded money from Johnny and Stephen. Johnny looked the man straight in the eye and barked,

"Back off." Discovering that he had just threatened Johnny Depp, the mugger tossed the bottle to the ground and said, "I ain't stealing from Captain Jack." But before the man could make a hasty retreat, Johnny handed him a few dollars and told him to "straighten out his life."[6] The man nodded apologetically and ran away.

Hopefully you haven't been mugged. But, at times, you may feel like you've been ambushed. Unexpectedly people say or do hurtful things, and you have to weigh your response. When that happens, try to measure your words and return hostility with hospitality. How different the world would be if more people made a practice of saying "I'm sorry" and "I forgive you"—and actually meant it.

KIND WAYS

1. Send a letter of apology to someone you may have hurt.
2. Release a small debt that someone owes you.
3. Using social media, restore a line of civil communication with someone who hurt you.
4. Encourage your family members to say, "I'm sorry"—even for the little things.
5. Find someone who has suffered an injustice and compliment them for the way they've risen above disappointment and disillusionment.

CHAPTER TWELVE

Manage the Conflict

As supportive as my hometown is, in my high school, there are people who would probably walk up to me and punch me in the face. There's a select few that will never like me. They don't like what I stand for. They don't like somebody who stands for being sober, who stands for anything happy. They're going to be negative no matter what.[1]

—Taylor Swift

With his daughter, Brittany Peck, on his arm, Todd Bachman did the unexpected on her wedding day. Escorting her down the aisle, he stopped, located Brittany's stepfather, and invited him to join them in the processional. That kind gesture—toward someone who had been an adversary—brought healing and peace to the family.

"In the beginning it was very difficult," Todd said, referring to his relationship with Brittany's stepfather. "We've had our highest of highs and lowest of lows. Years of dealing with lawyers and courts. But being able to put all that behind us and work on what's most important . . . it's a beautiful thing."

The stepfather agreed, saying, "That was the best day of my life. We have become family [again], and the children's needs . . . come first."[2]

Just because disagreements arise— and some people don't like you—doesn't mean that you're to be unkind or contentious.

It's impossible to agree on everything. But just because disagreements arise—and some people don't like you—doesn't mean that you're to be unkind or contentious. Sooner or later, however, someone will rub you the wrong way and you may say something you wish you hadn't. That's life. And, as much as you wish every dispute could be fixed with "I'm sorry," sometimes all you can do is manage the tensions.

Here are five steps you can take to give peace a better chance:

1. *Keep it together.* In *Mockingjay*, of the Hunger Games series, Finnick Odair says, "Better not to give in to it. It takes ten times as long to put yourself back together as it does to fall apart."[3] If a conflict is brewing, carefully consider whether the issue is worth a confrontation. And remember, reestablishing peace is usually more taxing and stressful than keeping peace in the first place.

2. *Choose love.* Martin Luther King Jr. said, "I have decided to stick with love. Hate is too great a burden to bear."[4] A kind life demands that we pursue peace and show love to our enemies: "If your enemy is hungry,

give him food to eat; if he is thirsty, give him water to drink" (Prov. 25:21 NIV).

If you've been mistreated, slandered, or marked as an enemy, you may be justified in defending yourself. But that usually just leads to more conflict. Sometimes it's better to remain silent or allow your friends to come to your defense. This is not a new idea. "If it is possible, as far as it depends on you, live at peace with everyone" (Rom. 12:18 NIV). So, how do you heal a strained relationship so the stress doesn't interfere with your sleep? First, realize that some disputes can be healed in one conversation—others may take months or years. Despite your apology or attempt to make amends, some people are bent on taking grudges to their grave. Second, call for a truce—even if there's nothing more you can say or do to turn an adversary into an ally. Third, make every effort to return aggression with love—and repay disrespect with honor. Your enemy may not respond with grace, but at least you can know you tried.

> *If a conflict is brewing, carefully consider whether the issue is worth a confrontation.*

3. *Show mercy.* Anyone can mete out punishment in the name of upholding justice. But sometimes the best chance for healing comes through grace and mercy.

Police Officer Mark Engravalle could have become Sarah's adversary. Instead she became the unofficial president of his fan club. Sarah was caught shoplifting diapers and shoes for her two-year-old twin daughters at a Walmart in Kansas City, Missouri. She had fallen on hard times after her husband died and didn't know where to turn for help. When Engravalle arrived to make the arrest, he noticed the two children were barefoot. When he asked Sarah to explain her actions, she tearfully shared her story. After issuing a citation, the officer marched inside the store and, using his own money, purchased the items the young mother needed.

"Obviously she is going through a tough time," Engravalle told *41 Action News*. Some "might see her as a criminal, but I just saw her as a mom going through a really difficult time."

When local television stations ran the story of the officer's kindness, the community responded with an additional $6,000 in donations for the family. Sarah said the outpouring of support restored her hope and gave her a new outlook on life. "There aren't enough words in the world to thank [the police officer]," she told *ABC News*. "Me and my girls are indebted to him forever."[5]

Don't allow days or weeks to pass before endeavoring to heal wounds caused by the dispute.

4. *Act quickly.* When conflicts arise—*and they will*—take immediate action. Try to reach a quick resolution or compromise. Don't allow days or weeks to pass before endeavoring to heal wounds caused by the dispute. Otherwise, minor bumps and bruises can become long-term injuries to the relationship. Seek to reconcile through respectful conversation and acts of kindness. If voices begin to escalate into a heated exchange, don't try to match decibels. Remain calm and composed. Mother Teresa said, "I have found the paradox, that if you love until it hurts, there can be no more hurt, only more love."[6]

5. *Hold a conversation.* Don't try to settle disputes through emails or texts. Meet face-to-face whenever possible. Don't allow a friendship or business relationship to suffer because you didn't take the extra step of connecting in person.

Whether you're negotiating a cease-fire in your family or circle of friends—or mending fences in a business relationship—your acts of kindness are never wasted. With a little good fortune and a dose of understanding, your adversary could one day become your most-trusted ally.

KIND WAYS

1. Go out of your way to greet someone you don't like.
2. If family members are embroiled in a disagreement, become a peacemaker by helping each side see the other's point of view.
3. Before pulling the trigger on a lawsuit, attempt one more time to settle the dispute out of court.
4. If friends are contemplating divorce, encourage them to explore whether professional counseling can help them repair the marriage.
5. Make a commitment not to add fuel to the fire by gossiping about those with whom you find yourself in conflict.

CHAPTER THIRTEEN

No Room for Favorites

It's just a sick cycle of . . . why we don't want kindness and unity, why we want hate and division. We don't want that, nobody wants that. . . . So, let's teach people that kindness and unity help you go a lot further in life.[1]

—Gina Rodriguez

SuEllen Fried, a grandmother in her eighties, isn't afraid to rub shoulders with murderers, drug dealers, and white-collar criminals. She spends her days teaching the power of kindness and empathy in Kansas's eighteen prisons.

"I'm addicted to personal transformations," SuEllen says. More than 90 percent of the inmates who complete her program do not return to prison. She centers her teaching on the importance of inmates building a new life based on helping others, especially people who have been abused, bullied, or marginalized.

Weekly meetings resemble an Alcoholics Anonymous session. With guidance, the inmates conduct the meetings themselves. Each session begins with group recitation of the following: *We believe that no one has the right to hit anyone. We believe in using alternatives to cope with stress and anger. We believe in advocating a violence-free lifestyle. We believe that, even though we are incarcerated, we can help those in need. We believe in the importance of caring for humanity.*

For thirty years, SuEllen has taught inmates the principles of kindness. She wears a pin that reads, "Power of Kindness." Whenever she sees people perform good deeds, she rewards them with an identical pin. "We need more than just random acts of kindness," she said. "We need intentional acts of kindness."[2]

Why would a grandmother dedicate her retirement years to helping inmates? Because she sees great value in people that others don't. And, through love and kindness, she believes every life is redeemable.

When you meet people who aren't like you, dig deep and find the courage to build a bridge. Make an effort to surprise them with your friendliness and acceptance. Look beyond their skin color, brands of clothing, political leanings, religious affiliation, lifestyle choices, and more. See people as opportunities to be kind. Look at those who are different as God's unique creations who are *equally* deserving of your love and respect. Don't allow fear to perpetuate isolation and segregation. Racism, sexism, and other forms of bigotry are perpetuated because bridges and friendships aren't built between races, genders, faiths, political parties, age groups, social classes, cultures, and more.

No Room for Favorites

Regrettably, some people propagate a "vision of division." They prefer to be isolated from those who aren't like them: the poor, the unpopular, and the disabled, for example. Others, like you and SuEllen, believe people deserve love and respect regardless of where they come from, how they look, or what they need. You want the best for *all* people. Whether it's a homeless man, runaway teenager, prostitute, drug addict, or white-collar criminal—you believe every life is important.

> **People deserve love and respect regardless of where they come from, how they look, or what they need.**

You may not agree with another person's politics or lifestyle, but spend your life working so that everyone is treated fairly. There's no justification for hate crimes, name-calling, or prejudice. Some have demanded more tolerance among races, religions, and political parties. But tolerance is a nonissue when you love, respect, and value another human being. Tolerance is temporary—and often forced. Love is never ending—and freely given.

One afternoon, Robert Pattinson, star of *Twilight*, exhibited love and respect for a forgotten man relegated to living on a Los Angeles sidewalk. The actor stopped to befriend the homeless man who was humming a tune and strumming a beat-up guitar. Robert didn't try to avoid eye contact by racing past him or dashing across the street. Instead he stopped to thank the man for his music, handed him a twenty, and then proceeded to his car. A few minutes later, Robert returned carrying a brand new acoustic guitar. One bystander told the *Sun* newspaper that when the actor handed the homeless man the instrument, the man was shell-shocked. "He had no idea who Robert was—I think he thought the guitar was stolen. He was looking left and right, half expecting the police to arrest him. But Robert quickly went back to his car and drove off."[3]

If you don't show kindness to someone, it's possible no one will.

It's become fashionable to talk about kindness. Many wear T-shirts and display bumper stickers that advocate love and peace. But, in their everyday lives, they actually practice selective kindness. They choose whom they help and befriend based on how they feel that particular day. They're driven by emotion and attitude, rather than by meeting another person's need. Their criteria would change, however, if they began to value each person as much as they do a family member.

Actress Rene Zellweger and comedian-actor Zach Galifianakis treated eighty-seven-year-old Elizabeth Haist as if she were their grandmother. After hearing she was living on tip money while volunteering at a California Laundromat, the two actors decided to offer a helping hand. With limited resources, Haist had bounced between friends' apartments for years and had no place to call home. So Zach rented her a small apartment and Rene agreed to furnish it. Since then, Haist has become an extended member of Zach's family. She has even accompanied him to several Hollywood premieres. "It's not something that I ever dreamed I'd experience," she said, "but I'll never forget it."[4]

Many deeds go undone . . . because acts of kindness are buried beneath a truckload of insecurity and trepidation.

If a voice inside your head says it's time to bolt from your comfort zone and befriend the lonely, feed the hungry, and comfort the weak—do it! Despite fears and doubts, do the right thing and extend a helping hand. After all, if you don't show kindness to someone, it's possible no one will. Many deeds go undone—and people go unloved—because acts of kindness are buried beneath a truckload of insecurity and trepidation.

Taking the first step or uttering the first word is the most difficult. But if you're able to cross that bridge, you might just discover that you have a lot in common. You may like the same music, dislike the same politicians, and enjoy the same food. Friendship may be closer than you think.

Is there someone right now you need to befriend? It could be a homeless person, reclusive neighbor, foreign-exchange student, senior citizen, disabled veteran, or coworker of a different ethnicity. Just take the first step and speak from the heart. In no time, defenses will come down and new friendships will be born. There's no reason to take evasive action. You have a secret weapon in your possession. You have the power of kindness.

KIND WAYS

1. Talk to a person at a work party, church gathering, or school activity who appears to be socially uncomfortable.
2. Introduce a new student or coworker to your friends.
3. Give up your seat on the bus to someone who's elderly, pregnant, or just plain tired.
4. Carry bottles of water in your car and hand them out to road and utility workers, passengers at a bus stop, or people who are homeless.
5. Leave an unexpected tip for a service provider: your landscaper, garbage collector, trainer, and others.

CHAPTER FOURTEEN

Don't Be a Spectator

At the end of the day it's not about what you have or even what you've accomplished. It's about what you've done with those accomplishments. It's about who you've lifted up, who you've made better. It's about what you've given back.[1]

—Denzel Washington

Actress, model, and singer Zendaya came to the defense of her parents after someone posted a photo of them on Twitter and made a derogatory remark. In her response, Zendaya kept her cool. She wrote: "First I'm gonna pray for you. While you're so concerned about what my parents look like, please know that these are two of the most selfless people in the world. They have chosen to spend their entire life, not worried about trivial things such as looks and insulting people's parents on Twitter, but instead became educators who have dedicated their lives to teaching, cultivating and filling young minds. (One of the most important yet underpaid jobs we have.) Please, log out, go to school, hug a teacher and read a textbook. And while you're at it, go look in the mirror and know that you too are beautiful, because such hateful things only stem from internal struggles. Bless you."[2]

Thousands of Twitter followers congratulated Zendaya for the way in which she defended her family. Joey Prusak's defense of a stranger was equally impressive. The manager at a Dairy Queen, Joey, nineteen, saw a man who was blind drop twenty dollars in the restaurant, which was picked up and pocketed by another customer. Joey confronted the woman, asking her to return the money. She said, "No, it's mine—I dropped it." The manager replied, "I'm not going to serve you if you're going to be disrespectful and steal someone's money." When the woman profanely refused, Joey ordered her to leave the store. But the employee didn't stop there. He reached into his wallet and retrieved a twenty-dollar bill and handed it to the blind man. "Sir," he said, "on behalf of Dairy Queen, I would like to give you the $20 you happened to drop on the ground as you walked away from the counter. It's not your $20 bill because a woman took it, but hopefully this makes things right."[3]

> *Sometimes kindness requires that you move from being an agitated spectator to being a fierce defender.*

When you hear stories of injustice, doesn't it make you want to take the law into your own hands? At times, you can probably imagine yourself smashing a cyber-bully's computer—or apprehending a thief. It's human nature to want justice. That's why your fists tighten when you hear a repairman overcharge an elderly couple. It's why your teeth clench when kids gang up on a smaller classmate. And it's why you shake your head when a supervisor verbally abuses an employee.

But sometimes kindness requires that you move from being an agitated spectator to being a fierce defender. It means taking a stand for justice by speaking up for people who are overmatched and outnumbered.

Whenever you see injustice, it's safer to ignore it and do nothing. When you raise your voice in defense of others, you put yourself at risk. Retreating will protect you temporarily, but that approach only perpetuates more injustice and suffering.

Don't allow the threat of retaliation to make you a spectator. When you see people oppressed—or see animals or the environment under attack—don't hesitate to take action. Remember, in that moment, you are the superhero. Take a stand for liberty and justice for all. "Learn to do good. Work for justice. Help the down-and-out. Stand up for the homeless. Go to bat for the defenseless" (Isa. 1:17).

At times, defending others requires more than words. Such was the case in Pendleton, Oregon, after two youths mocked a seventy-five-year-old man seated on his veranda. "Look at that crappy house," they yelled. "They just need to burn it down." A railroad worker, John Cyganik, thirty-five, overheard their rude comments and saw the homeowner, Leonard Bullock, lower his head in shame. "I thought about saying something to the boys," John said, "but sometimes anger is better left unsaid. I took a different course of action that ended up paying off more than if I had yelled at them."

John persuaded a local hardware store to donate paint and used social media to recruit more than one hundred volunteers to refurbish the house. A local lumberyard even built a new porch and roofers repaired some leaks. Several residents joined together and purchased a new set of patio furniture and a local coffee shop donated iced tea for the workers. Leonard was so elated that he could hardly speak. "The house is real nice now," he told *ABC News*. "It makes me feel good to look at it, especially after what the teenagers said."

> *Injustice sneers back at you and dares you to respond. In a heckling tone, it says, "Don't get involved—it doesn't concern you."*

"Yeah, it was a random act of kindness," John told the *Union Pacific* blog. "But to me it's more about respect. I was raised to respect the people who came before you, to help others out who don't have much. Leonard can now sit on his front porch for the rest of his years while feeling good about his home."[4]

As John discovered, injustice sneers back at you and dares you to respond. In a heckling tone, it says, "Don't get involved—it doesn't concern you." But, as Robert F. Kennedy said in the 1960s, justice and kindness are everyone's business: "Each time a man stands up for an ideal, or acts to improve the lot of others, or strikes out against injustice, he sends forth a tiny ripple of hope, and crossing each other from a million different centers of energy . . . those ripples build a current which can sweep down the mightiest walls of oppression and resistance."[5]

> *It's voices like yours—not vigilantes—that will protect the poor, disabled, elderly, and marginalized.*

The nation still clamors for justice. Many still suffer at the hands of oppressors. But it's voices like yours—not vigilantes—

that will protect the poor, disabled, elderly, and marginalized from further exploitation. From a heart of kindness, will you stand and say, "There are no second class citizens—nor should anyone be made to feel like one. Every life is precious to God and must be treasured, because 'injustice anywhere is a threat to justice everywhere'[6]"?

Remember, your voice is a vote for justice; your silence may be interpreted as a vote for injustice.

KIND WAYS

1. Throw a party at an orphanage or nursing home.
2. Report bullying on social media to the appropriate authorities.
3. Adopt a pet from the Humane Society.
4. Support Special Olympics.
5. Run a 5k for organizations such as the National Breast Cancer Foundation.

CHAPTER FIFTEEN

Throw a Banquet

Is the rich world aware of how four billion of the seven billion live? If we were aware, we would want to help out, we'd want to get involved.[1]

—Bill Gates

It was supposed to be the happiest day of Quinn Duane's young life. For her wedding reception, an elegant room at a swanky hotel had been rented. A four-star gourmet meal was paid for and meticulously planned. Quinn's perfectly fitted designer dress had also arrived. And hundreds of relatives and friends had sent RSVPs. Everything was in place for a wedding people would be talking about for years. But just five days before the ceremony, the groom suffered cold feet and called off the wedding.

With more than $35,000 spent on the reception, Quinn decided to make the most of her "nonrefundable" situation. She phoned a local homeless shelter and invited residents to enjoy a hot meal at the Citizen Hotel in Sacramento, California, on her would-be wedding day.

That afternoon, the reception hall was filled with single parents and their toddlers, unemployed workers, displaced families, and young people who had lost their way. Like royalty, they were ushered to tables draped with linen tablecloths and adorned with fine china. Uniformed waiters and waitresses served gnocchi, salmon, steak, and more. It was a meal fit for a monarch's wedding. Despite her disappointment, embarrassment, and pain, Quinn found the strength to do something nice for a room full of strangers.[2]

Do you remember pulling up to a stoplight where a man or woman was holding a sign that read, "Hungry, will work for food"? Perhaps you tried to avoid eye contact as you debated whether to donate a few dollars. Finally you rolled down the window and the rapid handoff culminated with "God bless you."

Driving past the homeless or closing your eyes to genuine needs . . . will only lead to more suffering and death.

Acts of kindness like these won't eradicate global hunger or put local food banks out of business. But they do meet real needs. Yes, some sign-holders aren't really hungry and are scamming well-meaning motorists, but many really do need assistance. If you stop to listen to their stories, you'll learn how they fell on hard times: jobs were lost, medical bills soared, crimes were committed, families were broken, and more. The truth is, despite the generous donations of people like you and the heroic efforts of relief workers, billions still live in poverty. Globally thousands die each day from malnutrition and diseases related to hunger and unclean water.

Recording artist Bono said, "Where you live in the world should not determine whether you live in the world."[3] The needs *are* overwhelming. But driving past the homeless or closing your eyes to genuine needs in developing nations will only lead to more suffering and death.

For decades, many assumed the solution to poverty in the United States could be found in government programs. But, unfortunately, citizens continue to fall through the cracks: children go to school hungry, the elderly are forced to cut back on medications, and women can't afford routine breast cancer screenings. Governments are realizing they can't do everything. They need people like you who feel a moral obligation to help others escape poverty. "Those of us who are strong and able in the faith need to step in and lend a hand to those who falter, and not just do what is most convenient for us. Strength is for service, not status. Each one of us needs to look after the good of the people around us, asking ourselves, 'How can I help?'" (Rom. 15:1).

President Franklin D. Roosevelt said, "The test of our progress is not whether we add more to the abundance of those who have much; it is whether we provide enough for those who have too little."[4]

Today the poor are not always homeless, unemployed, or collecting welfare. The "working poor" may be your next-door neighbor or the person sitting across from you at a fast-food restaurant. It could be the person mowing your lawn or bagging your groceries. Each month, they stand in line for food programs and pray their utilities won't be turned off. Meanwhile, they dream of a fresh start: a well-paying job, school clothes for their children, a car without dented fenders and bald tires, a visit to the grocery store without having to count pennies, and a house they can call their own. With just a little help and kindness from friends like you, that dream could come true for millions across the nation and around the world.

They are not looking for lectures—they just want to know you care enough to learn their names and ask what they really need.

You may be asking, "What can I *really* do to make a difference?" Begin by exploring how you can assist an effective and reputable charity, church, or agency in your community. There are also national and international organizations deserving of your support. But, if you're willing to help people climb out of poverty, don't be surprised if opportunities actually find you: perhaps sponsoring a child each month in a feeding program, connecting a homeless family to housing and employment services, volunteering at your local food bank, or just feeding the hungry as they come across your path.

Regardless of how you help people living below the poverty line, allow them to maintain their dignity. They don't need you to pity them, as if you're in some way superior. Rather, you need to communicate from a place of friendship, humility, and sincerity. Once your motives are trusted, your counsel will be valued. They are not looking for lectures—they just want to know you care enough to learn their names and ask what they really need.

The eradication of poverty may not be accomplished in your lifetime. But many of the symptoms *can* be treated, including hunger and a lack of education, health care, shelter, and water. The key to addressing these problems is willpower and participation. As Bono said, "If you want to eliminate hunger, everybody has to be involved."[5] Actress Jennifer Aniston, star of *Friends* and *Cake*, also pledged to do her part: "I have more than everything I could ever need," she said. "I want to give others [what] they need."[6]

Few have the wealth and name recognition of Bono and Jennifer, but you have an equally important role to play.

Children scavenge for food off garbage heaps, women sell their bodies in the streets, and men hold signs on street corners.

Right now, children scavenge for food off garbage heaps, women sell their bodies in the streets, and men hold signs on street corners. Their future rests on the kindness of people like you. Obviously, you don't need another guilt trip laid on you. But, during your lifetime, make it your mission to do something great—help someone break out of the cycle of poverty.

KIND WAYS

1. Volunteer to serve at or support a homeless shelter.
2. Participate in a food-packing party for organizations such as Feed My Starving Children and Meals from the Heartland.
3. On special holidays like Thanksgiving and Christmas invite a less fortunate family to join you for a meal.
4. Start a drive to collect toys at your work, school, or church for Toys for Tots.
5. Travel to a developing nation or a downtrodden community to more fully understand the urgent human need.

CHAPTER SIXTEEN

Are You Prepared?

When you face a crisis, you know who your friends are.[1]

—Magic Johnson

The Los Angeles Dodgers had just lost their fourth straight game to the San Francisco Giants at AT&T Park on the Bay. Fans were cheering the home team and jeering the Dodgers as they filed off the field. Batboys hurriedly stuffed bats into duffel bags for the flight home. Grounds crews raked the infield. And upstairs in the press box sportswriters pounded away on their computers. No one noticed that Matt Kemp, then star outfielder for the Dodgers, had jogged down the left field line to meet with a fan and his father.[2]

Matt didn't need to introduce himself to Joshua Jones, nineteen, but he did anyway. He shook Joshua's hand and gave him a signed baseball. But Matt didn't stop there. He removed his cap and handed it to Joshua. Then he shed his jersey and cleats and gave them to Joshua too. He shook the young man's hand a final time and told him to "hang in there," before running off the field in what was left of his uniform.[3]

Joshua sat there stunned and speechless.

Later, Matt explained his actions: "Honestly I didn't know anyone was filming it. Our third base coach told me there was a big Dodger fan at the game who didn't have long to live, so I decided after the game to go over and meet him. I thought it might cheer him up and help him out a little bit. Life is so much bigger than baseball."[4]

A few months later, Joshua died of cancer. But, before he passed, he posted a photograph of the gear Matt had given him, along with the following message: "Matt Kemp gave me his uniform! Thanks Matt, I will never forget that moment!!!"[5]

> *When people are at their lowest, they need you to be at your kindest.*

When people are at their lowest, they need you to be at your kindest. Being considerate and nice is not always enough. Sometimes—as Matt demonstrated—kindness means going beyond a handshake and a smile and doing something extraordinary to show your love and support. When people are on the operating table, so to speak, your response can make the difference between hope and hopelessness. It's in those moments—when a person's world seems to be crashing down—that you can help them believe a better future is within their grasp.

Often, crises enter your orbit unannounced: a family member suffers a heart attack, a friend is arrested for a DUI, a co-worker's spouse files for divorce. To offer the right prescription of hope and encouragement, you need to be emotionally and spiritually prepared. College basketball coach John Wooden said, "When opportunity comes, it's too late to prepare."[6] Are you preparing? Are you anticipating your opportunity to make a difference in someone's life? And when you get that chance, will you be ready?

Actress Mila Kunis was prepared. She had hired a contractor to do some work in her home. But in the middle of the job, he suffered a violent seizure. Mila leaped into action by raising the man's head and sitting on the floor with him until the paramedics arrived. "You're going to make it," she said repeatedly. "Everything is going to be all right." Mila's compassion kept the man's hope alive and may have saved his life.[7]

You are uniquely equipped to help others through their crises.

Most people want to help others cope with the crises of life, but they're afraid they'll say or do the wrong thing. So, regrettably, they back away at a time when a kind and thoughtful friend could help accelerate the healing process. Your small and seemingly insignificant acts of kindness can help people overcome huge obstacles. Perhaps you already know the pain of sickness, broken relationships, job loss, eating disorders, and the like. If so, then you are uniquely equipped to help others through *their* crises.

The following five principles will help you show kindness to others when hardship comes their way:

1. *Grieve with them.* You may not be able to remove the crisis or take away the pain, but you can share the burden. Do not be afraid to shed tears of your own. Remind them that grief is medicine and tears are therapeutic.

113

2. *Gather the right people.* A young single mother with three boys was asked what she learned after enduring thirty-three chemo treatments for breast cancer. She replied, "It taught me a new level of kindness—a kindness which allows others to show *you* kindness. . . . Because I chose to receive kindness, it built closer and new friendships."[8] Having some time alone for meditation and reflection is healthy, but the temptation is to drift away from people altogether. Hibernation is not the answer. Rather, help them gather with the right people.

3. *Encourage giving.* As family members and friends recover from crises, encourage them to look for ways to help others. Wounds from a crisis may last a lifetime, but at some point the grieving needs to end and the giving needs to begin. In giving they will find healing. "Praise be to . . . the God of all comfort, who comforts us in all our troubles, so that we can comfort those in any trouble with the comfort we ourselves receive from God" (2 Cor. 1:3–4 NIV).

4. *Provide perspective.* You may have physical or emotional scars of your own, which serve as a reminder of what you've been through. No life experience should be wasted, because crises teach patience, empathy, and perseverance. Don't hesitate to pass along the lessons you've learned to a friend or family member who is searching for understanding.

5. *Pray for them.* Many have discovered the power of prayer and witnessed how it can bring healing, unity, and restoration. In times of difficulty, it's a reminder that God is on your side. Even if you aren't sure he's listening,

your prayers send a message that you care. "Pray for your brothers and sisters. Keep your eyes open. Keep each other's spirits up so that no one falls behind or drops out" (Eph. 6:18).

Actor Mark Wahlberg doesn't wait for a crisis before praying for his family and friends. It's part of his daily routine. Mark told the *Catholic Herald*: "The first thing I do when I start my day is, I get down on my hands and knees and give thanks to God. . . . If I can start my day out by saying my prayers and getting myself focused, then I know I'm doing the right thing. That 10 minutes helps me in every way throughout the day. . . . I want to serve God and to be a good human being and to make up for the mistakes I made and the pain I put people through. That's what I'm praying for, and I recommend it to anybody."[9]

Many communities have come together to pray for peace and comfort in the wake of a terrorist attack or tragedy. In San Bernardino, California, for example, thousands gathered in San Manuel Stadium to mourn fourteen shooting deaths and to remember twenty-one others who were wounded.[10] Similar prayer vigils took place in cities such as Paris, Boston, Brussels, and more, where people gathered strength from their faith and each other. Prayer can sustain hope in the face of danger.

In times of crisis or hardship, follow your instincts and simply do what you can. Liz Korsearas, a twenty-three-year-old IT administrator, took that approach when responding to the Boston Marathon bombing. She demonstrated that when you do what you can, it becomes a catalyst for others to do what they can.

When Liz saw reports of the Boston Marathon tragedy, she wanted to respond in a tangible way. She posted a message online, encouraging people to join her in buying pizzas for people who were housing stranded runners. Within forty-five minutes, hundreds of people from across the country, Canada, Puerto Rico, Barbados, and more offered to help. Although she was based in California, she found herself coordinating pizza deliveries to shelters, hospitals, fire departments, and police departments on the East Coast.

Your simple acts of kindness will never be forgotten.

Liz contacted Anytime Pizza, a restaurant located in Cambridge, Massachusetts, and spoke to the co-owner, Perry Silveira. Initially he was skeptical—he couldn't believe people across the country would be willing to sponsor pizzas. But once he caught the vision, he developed an action plan. He called his partner and told him he didn't care how much it cost—they were going to feed people. He said, "We're just going to cook all day, and send the food out to hospitals, fire departments, police departments and shelters."

Perry and his staff of twelve worked all night until finally, at 5:30 a.m., all their supplies were exhausted. They delivered hundreds of pizzas, salads, drinks, and more. The following day, Perry's team continued the effort, delivering to new locations—with or without pizza sponsorships.[11] Together, Liz and Perry showed how an act of kindness in times of crisis can deliver hope and bring out the best in people.

Make it your goal to do more for your friends and family members than they do for you. When they're facing hardship, make an effort to be by their side. They may not know how to ask for help, so don't be afraid to be proactive: lead them

116

in prayer, deliver a meal to their home, take their children to a movie, wax their car, or wash their dishes. In difficult circumstances, your simple acts of kindness will never be forgotten. Your family and friends will remember how they leaned on you. And, the next time you face a challenge, you can bet they'll be there for you too.

KIND WAYS

1. Volunteer at a local children's hospital.
2. Send flowers and a card to someone going through a difficult time.
3. Become a volunteer trained counselor for emergency services in your community.
4. Help someone search for a lost pet by posting signs and checking local shelters.
5. If you see a car on the side of the road, pull over and offer assistance. (Use caution and discretion.)

CHAPTER SEVENTEEN

A Vote for Civility

We pick politicians by how they look on TV and Miss America on where she stands on the issues. Isn't that a little backwards?[1]

—Jay Leno

In 1948 the South African government introduced apartheid, which restricted freedom and opportunities for nonwhites. In protest, Nelson Mandela began organizing nonviolent demonstrations against the government's oppressive, segregationist policies. Flexing its muscle, the government sentenced him to life in prison.

At his trial, Mandela said, "I have cherished the ideal of a democratic and free society in which all persons live together in harmony and with equal opportunities. It is an ideal which I hope to live for and to achieve. But if needs be, it is an ideal for which I am prepared to die."

The government's policies and Mandela's imprisonment sparked years of widespread protest and civil disobedience. By 1990, the back of apartheid was finally broken, and South

African President Frederik de Klerk ordered the release of Mandela, who had spent twenty-seven years in prison.

The world watched as Mandela and de Klerk shook hands, vowing to work together to end apartheid and promote reconciliation. Many who had supported the old apartheid regime and accused Mandela of terrorism began to actually admire him.

In 1994, in South Africa's first democratic vote, Mandela was elected president. He called on his fellow citizens—both black and white—to choose a path of forgiveness. He said, "If there are dreams about a beautiful South Africa, there are also roads that lead to their goal. Two of these roads could be named Goodness and Forgiveness. . . . No one is born hating another person because of the color of his skin, or his background, or his religion. People must learn to hate, and if they can learn to hate, they can be taught to love, for love comes more naturally to the human heart than its opposite."[2]

Unfortunately, political quarrels have spilled over into workplaces, classrooms, and communities.

Mandela learned that conflict and division are choices—even in a tough business like politics. But citizens have come to expect rancor and gridlock in the nation's capital, with "red" and "blue" pitted against one another. Unfortunately, political quarrels have spilled over into workplaces, classrooms, and communities. Once-friendly conversations have become partisan confrontations. It's likely that the divisive tone will persist unless citizens like you take steps to restore a sense of respect, cooperation, and decency to the corrosive world of politics.

Here are three ways you can take a stand for civility and kindness:

1. *Change the channel.* Political advertisements and talk shows have become weapons in a battle for public opinion. Twenty-four hours a day, partisans clash like gladiators intent on demonizing and destroying the competition. It would be easy to blame the networks for peddling antagonism on the airwaves. But television ratings are high because millions are watching. That won't change until people like you change the channel.

   Twenty-four hours a day, partisans clash like gladiators intent on demonizing and destroying the competition.

   Billions of dollars are spent each election cycle on negative advertising because political gurus contend they are more effective. The public, however, has the power to render them ineffective. Rather than yelling back at the television and raising your blood pressure, what if you declared your home a "demilitarized zone" and refused to watch negative programming? There are certainly less stressful ways to stay informed.

2. *Cherish the institution.* Regardless of your party affiliation, be sure to maintain a reverence for the US Constitution and the Declaration of Independence. The founding fathers paid a high price to establish the nation on the principle of "liberty and justice for all." Disdain for an opposing party or an elected official doesn't justify disparaging the entire institution. Kindness means showing proper respect for a governmental

office, even if you dislike the person filling a particular seat.

Leading up to election night, news media polls and projections often discourage voter turnout. But every citizen has a responsibility to be informed and to cast a vote. How can persons stand for civility and kindness in the political arena if they disengage from the process altogether? Recording artist Moby said, "It's heartbreaking that so many hundreds of millions of people around the world are desperate for the right to vote, but here in America people stay home on election day."[3]

As an advocate for a kinder society, you step into the voting booth with an added agenda.

As an advocate for a kinder society, you step into the voting booth with an added agenda. Obviously you're interested in a particular set of issues, but you're also committed to voting for candidates who will help change the political tone and represent values of civility and cooperation. You're not swayed by rehearsed speeches and empty promises. You simply want a candidate who will place the needs of the people above his or her political ambitions.

3. *Cooperate and compromise.* Contrary to popular opinion, don't be afraid to discuss politics in public. Demonstrate that it's possible to disagree without becoming disagreeable. Look for common ground and learn to work together with people who do not share your political perspective. Demand the same from your elected officials.

Some representatives are notorious for compromising personal convictions and casting votes for political advantage. Voting the party line has sabotaged many attempts at cooperation and compromise. Yet, throughout the nation's history, Americans *have* demonstrated the ability to come together to accomplish a common goal. Such was the case in 1863, when the government set out to build the first transcontinental railroad.[4] Many said the vision of laying nearly two thousand miles of track across rivers, canyons, and mountains was impossible. But elected officials and thousands of laborers from many different businesses came together to meet the challenge. Six years later, the final rail was laid, connecting the Pacific coast to a network of eastern rail systems. When completed, the travel time from one coast to the other was reduced from several months to seven days.

If elected officials could build the transcontinental railroad, they can work together to solve many of the problems plaguing the nation today. Take the time to write your elected officials, encouraging them to promote an atmosphere of cooperation and compromise. Ask them to set an example of goodwill and understanding for future generations. And don't be afraid to tell them they won't be getting your vote unless they do.

KIND WAYS

1. Write letters of appreciation to your elected officials who appear to be serving the people.
2. When your elected official appears to cross the line of civility, call his or her office and voice a complaint.

3. Be respectful of others' views when entering into political discussions with friends and coworkers.

4. Don't assume public officials are aware of problems in your state or community—let them know.

5. Turn off the radio and television news talk shows when the yelling begins.

CHAPTER EIGHTEEN

Protect and Save

If we're . . . destroying our environment and hurting animals
and hurting one another . . . there's got to be a very powerful
energy to fight that. I think we need more love in the world.
We need more kindness, more compassion, more joy, more
laughter. I definitely want to contribute to that.[1]

—Ellen DeGeneres

An estimated one hundred million tons of debris is floating
in the oceans.[2] According to Fabien Cousteau, grandson of
famed ocean explorer and oceanographer Jacques Cousteau,
one patch of garbage in the Pacific is larger than Canada.
Fabien, an aquatic filmmaker and oceanographic explorer,
finds that unacceptable.

To improve the health of the planet's oceans, Fabien has
spent years researching sharks, repopulating species of fish,
and bringing awareness to conservation. Perhaps one of his
most effective strategies for protecting the oceans involves
a simple marble.

> *Most agree that humans have never wielded as much power over the planet as now—nor posed as great a threat.*

"I carry a blue marble around with me," Fabien said, "because it's a symbol of our planet. It reminds me of our interconnectivity with our ocean world." But every day he makes it his goal to also give one marble away and to pose a challenge to the recipient: "You have one mission," he says, "to do one random act of kindness for the oceans in the next 48 hours. It's up to you to figure out what that is and then pass [the marble and challenge] on to someone else."[3]

Fabien's message is simple: everyone has a responsibility to be kind to the planet.

Even without a consensus on the greatest threat to the environment, most agree that humans have never wielded as much power over the planet as now—nor posed as great a threat. Experts don't fully understand the short- and long-term effects of that influence, but according to scientist Calvin DeWitt there is strong evidence for seven degradations of Earth that deserve your attention:[4]

1. Land is being converted from wilderness to agricultural acreage—and from agricultural acreage to urban areas—at an ever-increasing rate.
2. As many as three species become extinct each day.
3. Land is being degraded by pesticides, herbicides, and fertilizers.
4. The treatment and storage of hazardous chemicals and waste is an unresolved issue.
5. Pollution has become a global problem.

6. The atmosphere appears to be changing due to pollution and an increase in gases.

7. Some cultures are being crowded out by the expansion of civilization.

Some argue that technology will rescue the planet. But technological advances will be hard-pressed to keep pace with resource consumption and population growth, let alone replenish what's already been damaged or destroyed. According to the United Nations, urban populations will see the addition of 2.9 billion by 2050.[5] And energy demands will increase by 55 percent by 2030.[6]

> *Technological advances will be hard-pressed to keep pace with resource consumption and population growth.*

The environment has become highly political, but it's up to you to make it deeply personal. Most agree that ecological problems will not be solved through legislation and treaties. It will require individuals to show kindness to the planet by making changes such as the following to their daily habits:

> *The environment has become highly political, but it's up to you to make it deeply personal.*

1. Turn off the lights. (In the United States alone, if people were to turn off two lights each day it would save more than five billion kilowatt hours of electricity every year.)

2. Open the windows rather than using air-conditioning.

3. Take shorter showers and turn the water off when brushing your teeth.

4. Recycle.
5. Use rechargeable batteries and energy efficient light-bulbs and appliances.
6. Plant a tree or a garden.
7. Ride a bicycle or walk to work or school.
8. Consider skylights or solar panels.
9. Reduce toilet water.
10. Shop with reusable bags.

One person's kindness to the environment *can* make a difference. Just ask volunteers who take part in a series of coast-to-coast roadside trash collection treks with the organization Pick Up America. Some days, with trash bags as their companions, they cover less than a mile. But 3,672 miles later, they often collect more than two hundred thousand pounds of trash.[7]

Many churches, schools, businesses, and civic organizations have adopted community beautification and cleanup projects. Efforts include mobilizing cleanup crews, establishing recycling centers, investing in clean water and agricultural initiatives, and building energy efficient facilities. In Millville, Delaware, for example, parishioners from seven churches work side-by-side picking up roadside litter. In Indianapolis, Rotary International mobilizes citizens and club members to clean streams, collect trash, plant trees and gardens, and more. And across the nation, many schools and universities have established environmental awareness clubs.

Pope Francis asserted that an attack on the environment is an abuse of power: "Any harm done to the environment . . . is harm done to humanity. We . . . believe that the universe is the fruit of a loving decision by the Creator, who permits man respectfully to use creation for the good of his fellow men and for the glory of the Creator; he is not authorized to abuse it, much less to destroy it."[8]

If you're led by kindness, you want to be kind to the soil to save a tree. You want to be kind to the oceans to save a fish. You want to be kind to the air to save a bird. And you want to be kind to all three to help save humanity.

KIND WAYS

1. Carpool whenever possible.
2. Don't overwater your lawn.
3. Make it a practice to pick up sidewalk trash.
4. Use recycled paper.
5. Keep your car serviced.

CHAPTER NINETEEN

Passing Grades

I'm going to college. I don't care if it ruins my career. I'd rather be smart than a movie star.[1]

—Natalie Portman

For years, janitor Ricky Spaulding faithfully swept floors, cleaned toilets, and collected trash at Anderson County High School near Lexington, Kentucky. The students decided it was time they showed their appreciation.

When students heard that Ricky had not seen his son in a year—and had never met his grandson—they secretly collected donations for a family reunion. Ricky's son, a soldier, was stationed in Italy. On a janitor's salary, traveling to Italy was not something he and his wife could afford. One student told CNN, "He has done so much for us and our school, we wanted to do something for him."

During an assembly, Ricky was called to the gymnasium. He was told he needed to clean up a spill. When he entered carrying a mop and bucket, students erupted in applause.

YOUR NEXT 24 HOURS

The principal, microphone in hand, invited a stunned Ricky to join him at center court. He presented the janitor with a garbage can filled with nearly $2,000 in donations.

Fighting back tears, Ricky said, "Words cannot describe the joy I feel right now and how thankful I am to all the students who made this possible."[2]

If you're a student at a university, vocational institution, or high school like Anderson County, you're in a place with unlimited potential for good. Many people have received much-needed help and encouragement because one student like you saw a need and did something about it. You may be young and inexperienced, but you have the power to ignite a campus-wide compassion movement. You don't have to be class president, valedictorian, head cheerleader, or starting quarterback. But you do have to lead by example. You can't watch from the sidelines.

You have the power to ignite a campus-wide compassion movement.

Author Malcolm Gladwell highlighted "the bystander problem" in his book, *The Tipping Point*. He described a student who staged an epileptic fit in his dormitory: "When there was just one person next door, listening, that person rushed to the student's aid 85 percent of the time. But when subjects thought that there were four others also overhearing the seizure, they came to the student's aid only 31 percent of the time."[3] In other words, when it comes to a compassion movement, don't look around for someone else to lead. It can begin with you and your friends. Together you can sponsor an inner-city kid to go to camp. You can beautify a park or refurbish a baseball field. You can distribute food and clothes to the homeless. The needs in your radius are significant, but solutions can begin with you and your classmates.

Don't let excuses get in the way. Sure, like everyone else, you have homework, a social life, sports, work, associations, and more vying for your time. After all, you're a student—not a social worker. But life only gets busier, and your list of commitments and obligations only gets longer. Now is the time to extend yourself. Remember, the goal isn't for you to do everything. The objective is for you to do your part—and to inspire other students to join you. Together you can change lives and restore hope.

Campuses are hotbeds for social change. What happens on your campus can influence the course of nations:

*Students can be inspired to do good or radicalized to wreak terror. . . . More students need to believe they **can** change the world through a lifestyle of kindness.*

students can be inspired to do good or radicalized to wreak terror. On your campus, they can learn the principles of generosity or the doctrines of greed. What students become is largely influenced by what they learn in the classroom and what they see in the lives of fellow students like you. Through your kindness and compassion, you can help shape the leaders of tomorrow. Your good deeds speak louder than words: "And don't let anyone put you down because you're young. Teach . . . with your life: by word, by demeanor, by love, by faith, by integrity" (1 Tim. 4:12).

Civil debate and critical thought are vital to the educational experience. Hopefully, you and your fellow students will find a balance between constructive criticism and condemning cynicism. The cynic sees an issue and simply throws up his or her hands. The critic sees a problem and seeks a solution. More students need to believe they *can* change the world through a lifestyle of kindness.

Here are seven ways you can foster friendliness and an atmosphere of kindness on campus:

1. Open doors for others and let them go first.
2. Say "Thank you" at least five times per day.
3. Introduce yourself to students you don't know.
4. Pick up stray trash.
5. Smile and wave at friends in the hallway.
6. Pay attention during class lectures.
7. Compliment someone's clothes, hair, or makeup.

Many of the social issues facing the United States would be eliminated if students in five thousand colleges and twenty-five thousand high schools across the nation were inspired to selfless service. Granted, that's difficult in a society that defines success by academic degrees, job titles, and pay stubs. Nevertheless, many students are accepting the challenge. Since 1977, students at Penn State University have raised $137 million to fight pediatric cancer.[4] Students at the University of Illinois at Chicago prepare sandwiches and distribute them to hundreds of homeless men and women each week. Students at UCLA formed a club "dedicated to spreading joy in hopes of creating a culture of kindness on campus and in the community."[5] Members perform random acts of kindness, including

You don't want to look back regretfully on your education someday and say, "I learned a lot, but I didn't do enough to help others."

group hugs, giveaways, notes of appreciation to staff and faculty, and assisting the elderly. A similar "kindness club" was established at Abraham Lincoln High School in San Francisco, where students participate in canned food drives, beach reclamation, zoo cleanup, and more.[6]

The increase in compassion clubs and charity fund-raisers are two indications students are rising to the challenge. Many are rejecting a doctrine of greed and self-centeredness. They want a society where no one is left behind and every life is valued. They have little interest in being voted "Most likely to succeed." They'd prefer to be voted "Most likely to serve."

If you're a student, don't wait until you've walked the graduation line to pursue a lifestyle of service. Your campus needs you now. You don't want to look back regretfully on your education someday and say, "I learned a lot, but I didn't do enough to help others." Instead take what Dr. Seuss said to heart: "Unless someone like you cares a whole awful lot, nothing is going to get better. It's not."[7]

KIND WAYS

1. Express your gratitude to a teacher who is having a positive influence on campus.
2. Offer to help a fellow student who is struggling with a particular class or project.
3. Befriend someone who doesn't share your political, religious, or social views.
4. Pass out cookies in the dorms.
5. Organize students to undertake a community project.

CHAPTER TWENTY

The Perfect Work Team

If a man is called to be a street sweeper, he should sweep streets even as Michelangelo painted or Beethoven composed music or Shakespeare wrote poetry.[1]

—Martin Luther King Jr.

In 2015, Google, Inc. set out to assemble the "perfect work team." Research had revealed that group projects were producing the highest profitability, so the company wanted to assemble the right combination of engineers to work together. They learned that work teams found more solutions, innovated better, and had greater job satisfaction. But Google wanted to know why some groups experienced higher efficiency than others. After extensive research, the company reported its findings: they discovered that "team culture" was the major factor in determining a work group's productivity. They learned that when team members were friends away from work—and built a level of trust in one another—they were also more effective on the job. More than any other factor, "psychological safety" was critical to the team's success. The best teams valued each member's opinion. No single person dominated group discussions. And the team had a "social sensitivity to how others in the group were feeling."[2]

> Whether you're at the top of the corporate ladder or feel like you're at the bottom of the food chain, you can influence the culture of your workplace.

In the end, Google discovered the economic value of kindness in the workplace. Interestingly, researchers from Harvard Business School, Yale School of Management, and the University of Pennsylvania's Wharton School arrived at a similar conclusion. Their study revealed that a kinder work environment tends to be more productive. It said, "When we take time to help out others, it increases our sense of efficiency, thereby boosting our perception of the time we have available."[3]

Whether you're at the top of the corporate ladder or feel like you're at the bottom of the food chain, you can influence the culture of your workplace. There's more to your job than hitting a deadline, collecting a paycheck, or meeting a quota. You have a responsibility to cultivate a positive, empathetic work environment. Here are three ways you can nurture kindness in the workplace:

1. *Be an example.* Your fellow employees are observant. They watch how you interact with your coworkers. If you're greedy, lazy, or difficult to work with—they know it. If you're kind and caring—they know that too. In a sense, you're under surveillance. No, you don't have to worry about security officers knocking on your office

door and confiscating your phone or computer. But the tone of your emails, phone calls, and hallway conversations contributes to your reputation. And what your coworkers see and hear determines if you will be a trusted friend or just another company employee. When you model kindness in the workplace, you become a person employees want on their team.

> *Your fellow employees are observant. . . . If you're greedy, lazy, or difficult to work with— they know it.*

2. *Be a friend.* Some of your coworkers could be secretly suffering. They may have chosen not to broadcast their pain, but their families are broken, their finances are upside down, and their health is failing. Their job is an escape from their difficult circumstances. They need someone like you to ask "How are you?" and to actually care about their answer. "Each one of us needs to look after the good of the people around us, asking ourselves, 'How can I help?'" (Rom. 15:2).

3. *Be a voice.* Although you cannot impose your values on a company, you *can* encourage your employer to achieve goals that go beyond profitability. In fact, your company may be looking for someone like you to help lead and identify worthy community projects. Be a voice for kindness and compassion, and together with your coworkers make your business a powerful force for good.

Many companies have taken a lead in fostering a kinder work environment and mobilizing employees to care for their community. When an EF-5 tornado hit Joplin, Missouri, in 2011, for example, Bass Pro Shops founder, Johnny Morris, and his employees served on the front lines, helping families recover and working with Convoy of Hope to distribute food, water, and supplies. They even organized a daylong festival featuring Nashville entertainers and NASCAR drivers, which raised $400,000 for the relief and recovery effort.[4]

You can be an advocate for this kind of compassion in *your* workplace. Make an appointment with your employer or human resources director and volunteer to lead a public service initiative. Remember, you're not there representing yourself. You're speaking on behalf of people who desperately need the help your company can provide.

> *It's easy to get stressed over success and to confuse your career with your life.*

When Steve Jobs attempted to recruit PepsiCo's CEO, John Sculley, to run Apple, Inc., he said, "Do you want to sell sugar water for the rest of your life? Or come with me and change the world?"[5] Jobs was right about a lot of things, but he missed on this one: you *can* sell sugar water *and* change the world. You can be a teacher, accountant, waitress, sales executive, custodian, engineer, pastor, and more *and* change the world. It's easy to get stressed over success and to confuse your career with your life. But your job doesn't define who you are. Your vocation is merely a stage from which you can influence the lives of coworkers and the heart of the company itself.

At times, you may feel like you're just a number—especially in larger corporations. But if you're dedicating forty hours a week to the company, it's up to you to make that time profitable for yourself, your coworkers, and your employer. Each week, make it your goal to earn both your paycheck and a reputation for kindness.

KIND WAYS

1. Praise someone at work for a job well done in front of other coworkers or his or her supervisor.
2. Offer to bring back a sandwich or coffee for a coworker.
3. Find a community enhancement project that could be adopted by your company.
4. Graciously answer the questions of new employees and invite them to lunch.
5. Trade shifts with coworkers when they need time off for personal matters.

CHAPTER TWENTY-ONE

Don't Let Go

I like to envision the whole world as a jigsaw puzzle. . . . If you look at the whole picture, it is overwhelming and terrifying, but if you work on your little part of the jigsaw and know that people all over the world are working on their little bits, that's what will give you hope.[1]

—Jane Goodall

James Doohan stormed the beaches of Normandy in World War II and then went on to play Scotty, chief engineer of the USS *Enterprise* on television's *Star Trek*. But, according to James, his greatest accomplishment was helping to save a woman's life.

The actor received a distressing letter from a fan who was contemplating suicide. James reached out and invited her to attend a convention in Indianapolis, where he was making an appearance. The two met face-to-face, and James did his best to offer encouragement. Still fearing for her safety, he invited her to attend his next convention two weeks later in St. Louis.

In the months that followed, James kept the invitations coming. In all, the woman attended eighteen conventions. Then, without warning, she vanished. Months passed and James didn't hear from her. No phone calls, emails, or letters. He feared the worst.

Eight years later, James received a letter from the fan thanking him for his compassion. She said she had found renewed purpose and had gone on to complete her master's degree. She wanted the actor to know his unwavering kindness had saved her life and given her hope.[2]

> *Occasional kindness has limited power. But relentless kindness has the power to restore, inspire, rescue, and unite.*

This story could have ended much differently if James had not persisted in showing the woman he cared. What motivated him to continue reaching out to a stranger, show after show? The actor understood that when people find themselves in a cavern of despair, it might be *your* relentless kindness that becomes their rope to freedom. Consequently, you can't let go. James kept the rope taut for eighteen shows. He kept the fan's hope alive until she was able to climb her way to safety.

Undoubtedly, you have family members and friends who are facing difficult circumstances too. Maybe a relationship unraveled, a job was lost, or a cancerous tumor was discovered. You wish you could snap your fingers and make the problem go away, but you know a pat on the back and a brief "hello" won't help them cope with their pain. They need a shoulder to lean on—and someone who will take the journey with them. They need to hear you say, "Listen, I'm here for you—I'm not going anywhere."

When you choose to persevere in kindness, you unleash an unstoppable force for good. Occasional kindness has limited power. But relentless kindness has the power to restore, inspire, rescue, and unite. "Don't ever get tired of doing the right thing" (2 Thess. 3:13 NIrV).

Helping people often requires perseverance and sacrifice. It takes dedication, for example, to mow the lawn of a senior citizen each month. It takes staying power to drive a neighbor's child to Little League practice five nights a week. And it requires commitment to give up your Saturdays to volunteer at the YMCA. When you persist in kindness, you provide lasting help to others and unlock a door to greater happiness and purpose for yourself.

When you persist in kindness, you provide lasting help to others and unlock a door to greater happiness and purpose for yourself.

Relentless kindness is contagious. When people see you go the extra mile to help others, they're inspired to follow your example. Such was the case in Detroit, Michigan, at a citywide Convoy of Hope festival. More than five thousand guests were waiting in line for the gates to open. They had come to receive a full menu of free goods and services: groceries, haircuts, medical and dental screenings, tennis shoes, backpacks for school, and much more. Some fifteen hundred volunteers were on hand from local churches, civic organizations, and businesses to serve the honored guests.

It was rainy and temperatures were plunging. Volunteers had come prepared with umbrellas, warm jackets, stocking caps, and gloves. But many of the guests did not own a coat and were shaking in the biting wind. While organizers debated whether to shut down the outreach, one volunteer refused to give up. Without any prodding or fanfare, he removed his coat and draped it around a shivering child. In the next few minutes, hundreds of volunteers followed his example and began removing *their* hats, coats, and scarves and giving them to the guests. Others began passing out umbrellas, pushing guests in wheelchairs under tents, and toweling off the wet hair of hundreds of children.

That day volunteers discovered the power of pressing on in the face of adversity. It would have been easier to close down the event and run for cover. But because of the volunteers' perseverance and sacrifice, thousands of families received much-needed help. Anyone can give up—anyone can walk away. But when you persist in kindness, you inspire others to help and stay too.

The challenges facing many communities are overwhelming: loneliness, exploitation, drug addiction, prejudice, poverty, child abuse, and more. Legislation and protest marches can accomplish only so much. Some problems will fade only when the love inside citizens like you becomes a stronger force than the hatred and selfishness in others. As Sam said in *The Lord of the Rings*, "There's some good in this world, Mr. Frodo—and it's worth fighting for."[3] You can join the fight for "good" by choosing to be relentless in your kindness and compassion.

One afternoon, a high school sociology teacher asked his students a probing question: "If everyone followed your example—and lived the way you do—would the world be a better place?" One student chuckled, "Yeah—if they followed me on Sundays." The class erupted in laughter. Unintentionally, the student made the teacher's point: occasional kindness will not change the world or spark a movement of compassion. Instead, it will require people like you who are determined to "overwhelm the world" with relentless kindness. As South African archbishop and Nobel Peace Prize winner Desmond Tutu said, "Do your little bit of good where you are; it's those little bits of good put together that overwhelm the world."[4]

At times, relentless kindness also requires restraint. When people develop a pattern of foolish behavior, for example, you don't want to become an accomplice to their misery. In other words, you want to avoid acts of kindness that encourage or enable destructive habits. Sometimes kindness is saying, "I care about you, but I can't help you right now." Don't feel guilty for taking that stance. Your love and compassion haven't wavered. Your job is to care—and hold on tight—but not to carry. Kindness sometimes means taking a

> *Fortunately, your kindness is not contingent on their gratitude.*

long-range view. To help people find healing and happiness, it may be necessary to take steps that are unpopular. At first, they may be agitated or give you the cold shoulder for not coming to their rescue, but those emotions will pass as long as they know you haven't given up on them.

Count on it—there will be days when you feel like you're being smothered by the needs of others—and entering a witness protection program sounds very appealing. After all, no one would have your phone number. No one would know where you live. You could finally focus on yourself and escape the needs of everyone else. But the truth is, you need people and they need you. Yes, it's disheartening when you make sacrifices on behalf of family and friends, and they don't appear to appreciate all you've done. You wash their car, pay their bills, serve as a taxi driver, take care of their pets, and more. And they don't even say "Thank you." Fortunately, your kindness is not contingent on *their* gratitude. Despite weariness and disappointment, you continue to offer help and show you care because it's the right thing to do. And, as James Doohan discovered, it's likely that you're having a greater influence on their lives than you realize.

Just keep going. Don't give up. And never let go.

KIND WAYS

1. If you have a friend who is struggling with anxiety or depression, set up a regular time to have coffee together.
2. Befriend an elderly person and make frequent visits to his or her home or senior center.
3. Volunteer to serve as an usher at your church, welcoming members and visitors as they enter.
4. Each month, drop an anonymous note of gratitude to a different service provider: your mechanic, garbage collector, physician, grocery clerk, and others.
5. Create a "piggy bank" for extra coins that will be given to your favorite charity.

CHAPTER TWENTY-TWO

The Decision

A single act of kindness throws out roots in all directions, and the roots spring up and make new trees. The greatest work that kindness does to others is that it makes them kind themselves.[1]

—Amelia Earhart

After working a twelve-hour shift at the medical center in Barre, Vermont, nurse Kathleen Connors stopped at L & M Diner and ordered her usual pancakes and hot chocolate. Nothing out of the ordinary happened until she went to pay her bill. As she waited at the cash register, she felt compelled to do something kind. Kathleen paid the tab for a family seated in the corner. The anonymous gesture brought her total bill to about forty dollars.

Kathleen didn't think about it again until she returned to the diner a few days later. The manager explained that her act of kindness had started a chain reaction. That day, at least forty-six patrons anonymously paid for other customers' meals.[2] The generosity of one off-duty nurse set many good deeds in motion. Her kindness was multiplied. She discovered that kindness is seldom followed by a period. One act of kindness can be the opening sentence in a volume of goodwill. In fact, one good deed can begin a story that never ends.

In the next twenty-four hours, your acts of kindness can start a chain reaction in *your* life too. One act of kindness can become a day of kindness. And one day of kindness can grow into a lifestyle of kindness. Out of a heart of gratitude, do the kind things in front of you . . . until they become who you are. That decision will change everything.

> *In the next twenty-four hours, your acts of kindness can start a chain reaction in your life.*

Do you remember the kind and thoughtful things others have done for you: the special gifts, unexpected compliments, free labor, listening ear, shoulder to cry on, the mentoring, and more? Do you remember how their acts of kindness made you feel? Throughout the next twenty-four hours, set a goal to make others feel the same way.

When Kathleen was asked why she decided to pay someone's tab, she said she wanted to express appreciation to a community that had shown her so much love. Her kindness was born out of gratitude. Likewise, if you're thankful for *your* blessings, then return kindness with kindness. By giving a hug, paying for a meal, delivering a bouquet of flowers, or sending a thank-you card—you're demonstrating that you don't take someone's kindness and generosity for granted. "You have been treated generously, so live generously" (Matt. 10:8).

The Convoy of Hope story is a testament to what can be accomplished when gratitude and generosity converge. The story could have ended tragically if the Davis family had not shown love and kindness to us four children following our parents' fatal auto accident. Out of anger and bitterness, we could have chosen a life of crime or greed. Instead, out of thankful hearts, a charity was founded that has brought help and hope to millions. When gratitude and generosity come together, there's no limit to what can be accomplished.

In *Reader's Digest*, Stacy Lee of Columbia, Maryland, recounted how a stranger, filled with gratitude, chose to be generous:

> I saw a dress in a consignment shop that I knew my grand-daughter would love. But money was tight, so I asked the storeowner if she could hold it for me. "May I buy the dress for you?" asked another customer. "Thank you, but I can't accept such a gracious gift," I said. Then she told me why it was so important for her to help me. She'd been homeless for three years, she said, and had it not been for the kindness of strangers, she would not have been able to survive. "I'm no longer homeless, and my situation has improved," she said. "I promised myself that I would repay the kindness so many had shown me." That day she paid for the dress, and the only payment she would accept in return was a heartfelt hug.[3]

When you decide to be led by kindness, you may be surprised by how many opportunities come your way in the first twenty-four hours. You won't have to manufacture them. Your eyes will be opened to both simple and profound opportunities to show someone kindness. Whether it's lending a listening ear or making a sacrificial donation, be ready to seize the moment.

Utah postal worker Ron Lynch seized an opportunity to show kindness while delivering mail one day. He noticed twelve-year-old Matthew Flores rummaging through a bin of junk mail filled with old newsletters and advertisements. When asked what he was searching for, the boy explained that his family couldn't afford books. He was just looking for something to read.

Lynch recommended a visit to the public library, but the boy said he couldn't afford the bus fare. At that moment, Ron decided to do something kind. He took to social media requesting books from his network of friends. Even he was astounded by the response. Almost overnight, the boy received thousands of books to choose from. With a wide smile, Matthew said, "I'm going to read every one of them."[4]

As Ron demonstrated, kindness is often an instant decision. In a matter of seconds, you may be asked to choose between involvement and indifference, generosity and selfishness, forgiveness and retaliation. But life is less complicated when, in advance, you make a decision to be led by kindness. Then, when opportunities arise, your first instinct is to say, "Yes—I'll do something."

Tona Herndon, seventy-eight, chose a life of kindness long before she was mugged in a cemetery. One afternoon, while visiting her husband's grave in Bethany, Oklahoma, an attacker stole her purse and $750. Fortunately, a surveillance video led to the capture of the culprit a few days later.

Tona assumed the purse and money were lost forever, until she received a phone call asking her to rendezvous in a public parking lot with a fifteen-year-old boy named Christian. She learned he was the arrested mugger's son.

With cameras rolling, Christian timidly approached Tona. "I'm sorry about what happened," he said, reaching for his wallet. "[My dad] gave me $250 for my band trip, but I'm not sure if it was yours or however he got it, but I'd feel bad if I didn't give it to you."

Tona received the money, saying, "I accept this, but I want you to take your band trip." With a long embrace, she handed the money back to Christian.

Wiping a tear from his eye, the boy shook his head in disbelief. "Thank you," he said. "Thank you so much."[5]

Tona rewarded the boy's honesty. But her generosity did more than send Christian on a band trip. She showed him that he didn't have to follow in his father's footsteps. He could take a different path—one that leads to greater happiness and purpose.

Contrary to popular opinion, happiness isn't like a video game. With each good deed, you don't earn more points and advance to a higher level of happiness. If it were based on a point system, happiness would be difficult to maintain. Fortunately happiness is the result of who you are—not just what you do. Your acts of kindness are an outward expression of the love and happiness that are in your heart. Whether your love comes from faith, character, or gratitude, you feel compelled to show kindness. You're not necessarily trying to earn happiness or manufacture fulfillment. Rather, because of your genuine love for people, you want them to find happiness too. No one is forcing you to meet others' needs or demonstrate that you care; you do it because you want to. You do it because it's who you are.

Perhaps you're just embarking on a life of radical kindness. If so, you may be saying, "I'm not sure I can live this way—I don't think I have enough love in my heart." Well, in the next twenty-four hours, why not give it a try? You have nothing to lose and everything to gain. Just begin by doing the kind things in front of you and see what happens.

You may be surprised by how much good you can accomplish in one day and the sense of fulfillment it brings you. Then, just keep going. With each act of kindness you will be watering a seed of love and happiness inside you. In time, good deeds will come more naturally, because they're an outward expression of who you've become.

> *There are no "kindness police" who will slap you on the wrist when you make a mistake or miss an opportunity.*

Your decision to pursue a lifestyle of kindness means you want to make the welfare of others a higher priority. You want to help others experience laughter, friendship, full stomachs, good health, and lasting hope. Along the journey, there will be times when you disappoint yourself and others. Perhaps you'll say or do the wrong thing—everyone does. Other days, you'll wake up with a rotten attitude and want to escape people altogether.

Be prepared to show yourself some grace. There are no "kindness police" who will slap you on the wrist when you make a mistake or miss an opportunity. Just keep doing what you know is right.

> *People will see a difference in your smile, in your words, and in your deeds.*

By making the decision to be led by kindness, everything will change in the next twenty-four hours. From this point on, each day will be a new adventure, filled with exciting opportunities to be a force for good. Your decision will change the way you see the world—and change the way others see you. People will see a difference in your smile, in your words, and in your deeds. Many will want to follow *your* example and choose a life of kindness too. Your decision will start a chain reaction that can ignite a movement of kindness. You can't change the world alone, but you can be part of a sea change and inspire others to join you. And together you can make the world a lot kinder than the way you found it.

Mark your calendar, because this is a date you'll never forget. As of today—everything changes.

KIND WAYS

1. Clean out your clothes closet and donate items to a local thrift store.
2. Be a designated driver when you go out with your friends.
3. Take a lonely person to the movies and ask a friend to do the same.
4. Send dessert anonymously to another patron when you're at a restaurant with instructions to "pay it forward."
5. Encourage your family and friends to give you Walmart gift cards for Christmas and distribute them to people in need throughout the year.

Notes

Chapter 1 Ask the Right Question

1. Natalie Roterman, "Lady Di Quotes: 20 Sayings to Remember Princess Diana on Her Death Anniversary," *Latin Times*, August 31, 2015, http://www.latintimes.com/lady-di-quotes-20-sayings-remember-princess-diana-her-death-anniversary-205349.

2. Zayda Rivera, "Couple Finds Out Paul Walker Bought Their Engagement Ring," *New York Daily News*, December 4, 2013, http://www.nydailynews.com/entertainment/gossip/couple-finds-paul-walker-bought-engagement-ring-article-1.1537567.

3. "The Paul Walker Foundation Is Fulfilling His Legacy, Passion for the Ocean and Spontaneous Good Will," The Paul Walker Foundation, http://the-paul-walker-foundation.myshopify.com/pages/l-e-g-a-c-y.

4. Karl Albrecht, "The Paradoxical Power of Humility: Why Humility Is Underrated and Misunderstood," *Psychology Today*, January 8, 2015, https://www.psychologytoday.com/blog/brainsnacks/201501/the-paradoxical-power-humility.

5. Kevin Lindsey, "John Wooden, Thank You for Being Such a Great Teacher," Bleacher Report, June 5, 2010, http://bleacherreport.com/articles/401655-john-wooden-thank-you-for-being-such-a-great-teacher.

6. "Jake Gyllenhaal's Random Act of Kindness," *Independent.ie*, May 27, 2016, http://www.independent.ie/woman/celeb-news/jake-gyllenhaals-random-act-of-kindness-26842566.html.

7. Allison Takeda, "Amy Adams Gives Up First-Class Seat for Serviceman on Her Flight," *US Weekly*, June 27, 2014, http://www.usmagazine.com/celebrity-news/news/amy-adams-gives-up-first-class-seat-for-soldier-on-her-flight-2014276.

8. "Keanu Reeves Gives Up Subway Seat, New Yorkers Don't Seem to Notice (VIDEO)," *Huffington Post*, December 9, 2011, http://www.huffingtonpost.com/2011/12/09/keanu-reeves-gives-up-subway-seat_n_1139228.html.

9. "Simon Sinek: Why Leaders Eat Last," YouTube video, 33:30, posted by 99U, December 4, 2013, https://www.youtube.com/watch?v=ReRcHdeUG9Y.

10. Mandy Oaklander, "Do Happy People Really Live Longer?," *Time*, February 11, 2016, http://time.com/4217052/do-happy-people-really-live-longer/.

Chapter 2 Get Off Your Own Back

1. "'You've Got to Find What You Love,' Jobs Says," *Stanford News*, June 14, 2005, https://news.stanford.edu/2005/06/14/jobs-061505/.

2. Augusta Falletta, "Kate Winslet Officially Wrote No Retouching into Her L'Oreal Contract," BuzzFeed, October 22, 2015, https://www.buzzfeed.com/augusta falletta/kate-winslet-wont-allow-herself-to-be-retouched-in-her-lorea.

3. Maria Yagoda, "Kate Winslet Preaches Body Positivity to Daughter Mia: 'We're So Lucky We Have a Shape,'" *People*, July 28, 2015, http://www.people .com/article/kate-winslet-running-wild-body-image.

4. John C. Maxwell, "5 Essential Principles for Adding Value to Others: 1—Self-Worth," *Intentional Living* (blog), January 14, 2016, http://blog.johnmaxwell.com /intentionalliving/5-essential-principles-for-adding-value-to-others-1-self-worth.

5. Joel Osteen, *Become a Better You* (New York: Howard Books, 2009), 3.

6. Frances Masters, "13 Quotes about Confidence to Help You Grow," The Fusion Model, https://www.thefusionmodel.com/13-quotes-about-confidence -to-make-you-grow/.

7. Mark Tabb, *Living with Less: The Upside of Downsizing Your Life* (Nashville: B&H, 2006), 22.

8. Andy Stanley, *Enemies of the Heart: Breaking Free from the Four Emotions That Control You* (Colorado Springs: Multnomah Books, 2011), 129.

9. "24 Awesome Kindness Quotes," Think Kindness, http://thinkkindness .org/24-awesome-kindness-quotes/.

10. Ted Turner, telephone interview with author Hal Donaldson, 1982.

11. Erwin Raphael McManus, "Elevate the Room," podcast audio, February 10, 2016, https://itunes.apple.com/us/podcast/mosaic-erwin-raphael-mcmanus /id142417894?mt=2.

Chapter 3 Be Their Miracle

1. Jeffrey I. Moore, "23 Motivating Stephen Curry Quotes on Success, Basketball & Faith," *Everyday Power* (blog), October 9, 2015, http://everydaypowerblog.com /2015/10/09/23-motivating-stephen-curry-quotes-on-success-basketball-faith/.

2. "Bus Driver Delivers Free Home-Cooked Meals," CNN, March 20, 2009, http://www.cnn.com/2009/LIVING/03/19/cnnheroes.jorge.munoz/index.html.

3. "24 Teary-Eyed Stories You Must Read about the Touching Kindness of Strangers," *Reader's Digest*, October 2015, http://www.rd.com/true-stories /inspiring/kindness-strangers/.

4. Ibid.

5. "The Nicest Thing I Have Ever Witnessed Someone Do for a Stranger," *Huffington Post*, November 11, 2014, http://www.huffingtonpost.com/kindness -blog/the-nicest-thing-i-have-e_b_6133404.html.

Chapter 4 When Less Is More

1. Stephanie Sarkis, "25 Quotes on Giving: Learn from These Greats What It Means to Give," *Psychology Today*, December 11, 2012, https://www.psychology today.com/blog/here-there-and-everywhere/201212/25-quotes-giving.ok.

2. Sydney Lupkin, "Woman Donates Kidney to Stranger, Starts Kidney Transplant Chain," *ABC News*, March 6, 2015, http://abcnews.go.com/Health/woman -donates-kidney-stranger-starts-kidney-transplant-chain/story?id=29440792.

3. Mitch Albom, *The Five People You Meet in Heaven* (New York: Hachette Books, 2007), "The Second Lesson."

4. Dacher Keltner, "The Compassionate Species," *Greater Good*, July 31, 2012, http://greatergood.berkeley.edu/article/item/the_compassionate_species.

5. Troy Moon, "Pine Forest Student's Act of Kindness Is Inspiring," *Pensacola News Journal*, September 17, 2015, http://www.pnj.com/story/news/2015/09/17 /pine-forest-student-kind-act/32557893/.

6. *Numbers and Trends: Foster Care Statistics 2014* (Washington, DC: U.S. Department of Health & Human Services, Children's Bureau, 2016), 2, https:// www.childwelfare.gov/pubPDFs/foster.pdf#page=3&view=Children%20in, %20entering,%20and%20exiting%20care.

Chapter 5 It's Not Expensive

1. "Oprah Winfrey Interview: America's Beloved Best Friend," Academy of Achievement, last revised July 13, 2012, http://www.achievement.org/autodoc /page/win0int-7.

2. Steve Hartman, "Boy Who Gave Soldier $20 He Found Wins High Honor," *CBS News*, March 25, 2016, http://www.cbsnews.com/news/on-the-road-boy -who-gave-soldier-20-he-found-wins-high-honor-medal-of-honor-myles-eckert/.

3. *Cast Away*, IMDb, http://www.imdb.com/title/tt0162222/?ref_=nv_sr_2.

4. Department of Economic and Social Affairs, Population Division, *The World Population Situation in 2014: A Concise Report* (New York: United Nations, 2014), http://www.un.org/en/development/desa/population/publications/pdf /trends/Concise%20Report%20on%20the%20World%20Population%20 Situation%202014/en.pdf.

5. "Goal 1: End Poverty in All Its Forms Everywhere," United Nations Sustainable Development Goals, http://www.un.org/sustainabledevelopment/poverty/.

6. United States Census Bureau, *Income and Poverty in the United States: 2014—Highlights*, September 2015, https://www.census.gov/hhes/www/poverty /data/incpovhlth/2014/highlights.html.

7. Mark J. Perry, "Today's New Homes Are 1,000 Square Feet Larger Than in 1973, and the Living Space Per Person Has Doubled over Last 40 Years," American Enterprise Institute, February 26, 2014, https://www.aei.org/publication/todays -new-homes-are-1000-square-feet-larger-than-in-1973-and-the-living-space-per -person-has-doubled-over-last-40-years/.

8. Jennifer Abel, "Too Much Stuff? The Self-Storage Industry Keeps On Growing," *Consumer Affairs*, December 2, 2014, https://www.consumeraffairs.com /news/too-much-stuff-the-self-storage-industry-keeps-on-growing-120214.html.

9. Dan Rafter, "Think There's a McDonald's on Every Corner? Try Counting the Number of Self-Storage Facilities Dotting the Country," *Real Estate Journal*, April 17, 2015, http://www.rejournals.com/2015/04/17/think-theres-a-mcdonalds -on-every-corner-try-counting-the-number-of-self-storage-facilities-dotting-the -country/.

10. Myriah Towner, "Waitress Pays Grieving Couple's Restaurant Check Herself after Hearing They Had Lost Their Baby Daughter Just a Month Ago," *Daily Mail*, June 8, 2015, http://www.dailymail.co.uk/news/article-3116209/Waitress -random-act-kindness-touches-grieving-parents-lost-baby-girl.html.

11. Mayra Cuevas and Jamie White, "Pilot Buys Pizza for Delayed Passengers," CNN, July 9, 2014, http://www.cnn.com/2014/07/08/travel/delayed -passengers-pizza/.

Chapter 6 Stop the Clock!

1. Rick Warren, *The Purpose Driven Life: What on Earth Am I Here For?* (Grand Rapids: Zondervan, 2012), 165.

2. Sarah Smiley, "Strangers Find, Return Deployed Service Member's Wedding Band to His Wife," *Huffington Post*, October 6, 2013, http://www.huffingtonpost .com/sarah-smiley/strangers-find-return-deployed-service-members-wedding -band-to-his-wife_b_3702170.html.

3. Ben Leubsdorf, "We're Working More Hours—and Watching More TV," *Wall Street Journal*, June 24, 2015, http://www.wsj.com/articles/were-working -more-hoursand-watching-more-tv-1435187603.

4. Leo Buscaglia, as quoted in Shawdon Molavi, "Too often we underestimate the power of a touch, a smile, a kind word, a listening ear, an honest compliment, or the smallest act of caring, all of which have the potential to turn a life around," *HOMES Clinic Student Blog*, September 25, 2015, http://www.homes-clinic .org/blog/2015/9/25/too-often-we-underestimate-the-power-of-a-touch-a-smile-a -kind-word-a-listening-ear-an-honest-compliment-or-the-smallest-act-of-caring -all-of-which-have-the-potential-to-turn-a-life-around.

5. Michael Pearson, "Mark Hamill Skips 'Star Wars' Appearance to Visit Sick Kids," CNN, December 24, 2015, http://www.cnn.com/2015/12/24/entertainment /mark-hamill-star-wars-children-hospital-feat/.

Chapter 7 The Power of "With"

1. Aaron Ben-Zeév, "Why a Lover's Touch Is So Powerful," *Psychology Today*, May 18, 2014, https://www.psychologytoday.com/blog/in-the-name-love/201405 /why-lovers-touch-is-so-powerful.

2. Tom Rinaldi, "High School Teammates Carry On," ESPN, August 6, 2009, http://espn.go.com/espn/otl/news/story?id=4371874.

3. Sara Barnes, "Compassionate 70-Year-Old Woman Calms Aggressive Stranger by Holding His Hand," My Modern Met, February 11, 2016, http://www .mymodernmet.com/profiles/blogs/elderly-woman-calms-aggressive-man-on -train.

4. Maia Szalavitz, "Shocker: Empathy Dropped 40% in College Students Since 2000," *Psychology Today*, May 28, 2010, https://www.psychologytoday.com/blog /born-love/201005/shocker-empathy-dropped-40-in-college-students-2000.

5. Michael Grothaus, "Sean Parker on Why the World Needs a New Social Network," *Fast Company*, April 25, 2016, https://news.fastcompany.com /sean-parker-on-why-the-world-needs-a-new-social-network-4004500.

6. Antoinette Bueno, "Adam Levine's Reaction to a 10-Year-Old Fan with Down Syndrome Will Make You Love Him Even More," *Entertainment Tonight*, March 4, 2015, http://www.etonline.com/news/160621_adam_levine_treats_fan _with_down_syndrome/.

7. Mother Teresa, Nobel Lecture, The Nobel Peace Prize, December 11, 1979, http://www.nobelprize.org/nobel_prizes/peace/laureates/1979/teresa-lecture.html.

Chapter 8 Take a Breath

1. "'Sahara' Interview: Matthew McConaughey," Hollywood.com, http://www .hollywood.com/general/sahara-interview-matthew-mcconaughey-57167750/.

2. Brooke Shunatona, "Barber Gives Homeless People Free Haircuts, Proves There Are Good People in the World," *Cosmopolitan*, July 14, 2015, http://www .cosmopolitan.com/style-beauty/beauty/news/a43300/streets-barber-nasir -sobhani/.

3. Courtney Martin, "Listening Deeply in a Distracted World," Center for Courage and Renewal, February 2, 2012, http://www.couragerenewal.org/listen ing-deeply-in-a-distracted-world/.

4. Robert MacLeod, "Donaldson's Turn: How a Troubled Kid Rose through Baseball to Become the People's All-Star," *The Globe and Mail*, July 10, 2015, http:// www.theglobeandmail.com/sports/baseball/how-a-troubled-kid-rose-through -baseball-to-become-the-peoples-all-star/article25414792/.

Chapter 9 Speak and Destroy?

1. Katie Armour, "Top 12 Audrey Hepburn Quotes," *Matchbook*, April 22, 2013, https://www.matchbookmag.com/daily/45-top-12-audrey-hepburn-quotes.

2. "Letters Left in London by Anonymous," *Kindness Blog*, November 17, 2014, https://kindnessblog.com/2014/11/17/letters-left-in-london-by-anonymous/.

3. "Nearly a Third of Early Adulthood Depression Linked to Bullying in Teenage Years," University of Oxford, May 29, 2015, http://www.ox.ac.uk/news/2015 -05-29-nearly-third-early-adulthood-depression-linked-bullying-teenage-years.

4. "Daily Dose," *Verily Magazine*, May 4, 2016, http://verilymag.com/2016/05 /kind-words-can-be-short-and-easy-to-speak-but-their-echoes-are-truly-endless.

5. Ryan Grenoble, "Restaurant Owner Noticed Someone Digging in Dumpster, So She Wrote Them a Powerful Note," *Huffington Post*, April 13, 2015, http://www .huffingtonpost.com/2015/04/13/pbj-restaurant-dumpster-trash-free-meal-okla homa-city_n_7055672.html.

6. Cameron Keady, "Kids Return the Love to 'Grandma in the Window' Who Waves to Them Daily," *Huffington Post*, October 26, 2015, http://www.huffington

post.com/entry/grandma-in-window-bus-driver-washington_us_562a8056e4b
0443bb563ef58.

Chapter 10 Welcome to Reality TV

1. "Some Random Observations on Parenthood," Together For Children, http://www.together-for-children.org/tips.html.
2. Caroline Bologna, "Dad and Daughter Celebrate Their Birthdays with 39 Random Acts of Kindness," *Huffington Post*, June 25, 2015, http://www.huffington post.com/2015/06/25/dad-daughter-birthday-acts-of-kindness_n_7659320.html.
3. "Reading 2: Daily Life at 83 Beals Street," Determining the Facts, National Park Service, https://www.nps.gov/nr/twhp/wwwlps/lessons/33jfk/33facts2.htm.
4. Scott Stump, "Little Girl's Birthday Wish Fulfilled with Stuffed Animal Donations to Hospital," *Today*, July 30, 2015, http://www.today.com/parents /little-girls-birthday-wish-fulfilled-stuffed-animal-donations-hospital-t35611.

Chapter 11 Remove the Handcuffs

1. Jessica Durando, "15 of Nelson Mandela's best quotes," *USA Today*, December 6, 2013, http://www.usatoday.com/story/news/nation-now/2013/12/05 /nelson-mandela-quotes/3775255/.
2. Dick Scanlon, "A Rays Pitcher Is Humbled by the Gift of Forgiveness," Yahoo Sports, May 10, 2015, http://sports.yahoo.com/news/rays-pitcher-humbled-gift -forgiveness-190422338—mlb.html.
3. "Lessons on Forgiveness from T. D. Jakes," National Public Radio, April 5, 2012, http://www.npr.org/2012/04/05/150062615/lessons-on-forgiveness-from-t-d-jakes.
4. Benjamin P. Chapman, Kevin Fiscella, Ichiro Kawachi, Paul Duberstein, and Peter Muennig, "Emotion Suppression and Mortality Risk over a 12-Year Follow-Up," abstract, *Journal of Psychosomatic Research* 75, no. 4 (October 2013): 381–85, http://dx.doi.org/10.1016/j.jpsychores.2013.07.014.
5. Ernest Ogbozar, "Martin Luther King Jr.," *Love & Forgiveness in Governance*, December 31, 2013, http://blogs.shu.edu/diplomacyresearch/2013/12/31 /martin-luther-king-jr/.
6. Gordon Smart, "Johnny Depp Rescues Babybird Singer Stephen Jones from Mugger with Broken Bottle," *Daily Telegraph*, May 3, 2010, http://www.dailytele graph.com.au/entertainment/johnny-depp-rescues-babybird-singer-stephen-jones -from-mugger-with-broken-bottle/story-e6frewyr-1225861769745.

Chapter 12 Manage the Conflict

1. J. Freedom du Lac, "Her Song: Talking Taylor Swift," *Washington Post*, PostRock, February 28, 2008, http://voices.washingtonpost.com/postrock/2008 /02/her_song_talking_taylor_swift_1.html.
2. Jenny G. Zhang, "Bride's Father Halts Wedding So Daughter's Stepdad Can Walk Down the Aisle with Them," My Modern Met, September 28, 2015, http://www.mymodernmet.com/profiles/blogs/brides-father-stops-wedding-to -invite-stepdad-to-walk-with-him.

3. Nicole Pomarico, "6 Heartbreaking Quotes from 'Mockingjay' That Remind You How Sad the Story Really Is," *Bustle*, November 21, 2014, http://www.bustle .com/articles/50483-6-heartbreaking-quotes-from-mockingjay-that-remind-you -how-sad-the-story-really-is.

4. "'Where Do We Go From Here?,' Delivered at the 11th Annual SCLC Convention," Stanford University, https://kinginstitute.stanford.edu/king-papers /documents/where-do-we-go-here-delivered-11th-annual-sclc-convention.

5. Kimberly Yam, "Policeman Buys Diapers, Shoes for Mom of 6 Who Was Caught Shoplifting," *Huffington Post*, July 13, 2015, http://www.huffingtonpost .com/entry/cop-buys-diapers-shoes-for-mom-who-shoplifted_us_55a3e500e4b 0b8145f730ed9.

6. Mother Teresa, as quoted in Jake Darnell, "Only More Love," *Full of Grace* (blog), University of Notre Dame, April 17, 2013, http://blogs.nd.edu/fullofgrace /2013/04/17/only-more-love/.

Chapter 13 No Room for Favorites

1. Celia Fernandez, "Exclusive: Gina Rodriguez on Being Bullied & What's to Come on 'Jane the Virgin,'" *Latina*, October 26, 2015, http://www.latina.com /entertainment/celebrity/gina-rodriguez-bullying-shirt.

2. Carolyn Gregoire, "This 80-Year-Old Is Spreading Kindness and Hope in the Most Unlikely Place," *Huffington Post*, September 16, 2013, http://www .huffingtonpost.com/2013/09/16/suellen-fried_n_3895084.html.

3. "Random Act of Kindness by Robert Pattinson," Look to the Stars, September 2, 2011, https://www.looktothestars.org/news/6875-random-act-of-kind ness-by-robert-pattinson.

4. Aly Weisman, "Zach Galifianakis Bought a Homeless Woman an Apartment— And Took Her to 'The Hangover III' Premiere," *Business Insider*, May 22, 2013, http://www.businessinsider.com/zach-galifianakis-bought-homeless-woman -an-apartment-2013-5.

Chapter 14 Don't Be a Spectator

1. "Denzel On Mentoring: 'We Are All Extraordinary,'" *Huffington Post*, March 28, 2008, http://www.huffingtonpost.com/2008/01/17/denzel-on-mentoring -we-ar_n_81867.html.

2. Kendall Fisher, "See Zendaya's Perfect Response to Internet Trolls Who Called Her Parents Ugly," E Online, August 28, 2015, http://www.eonline.com /au/news/690795/see-zendaya-s-perfect-response-to-internet-trolls-who-called -her-parents-ugly.

3. Megan Griffo, "Dairy Queen Employee Goes Above and Beyond for Blind Customer," *Huffington Post*, September 16, 2013, http://www.huffingtonpost .com/2013/09/16/random-act-of-kindness_n_3936560.html.

4. Ryan Grenoble, "Community Comes Together to Repaint Man's House after Teens Laugh at It," *Huffington Post*, August 11, 2015, http://www.huffingtonpost .com/entry/josh-cyganik-paint-house_us_55ca155be4b0923c12be21f7.

5. Mark Memmott, "Looking Back: RFK's 'Ripple Of Hope' Speech in South Africa," National Public Radio, June 30, 2013, http://www.npr.org/sections /thetwo-way/2013/06/30/197342656/looking-back-rfks-ripple-of-hope-speech -in-south-africa.

6. Martin Luther King Jr., "Letter from a Birmingham Jail," April 16, 1963, https://kinginstitute.stanford.edu/king-papers/documents/letter-birmingham -jail. This is a draft made available by The Martin Luther King, Jr. Research and Education Institute, Stanford University.

Chapter 15 Throw a Banquet

1. "Philanthropy Quotes," National Philanthropic Trust, http://www.nptrust .org/history-of-giving/philanthropic-quotes/.

2. Danute Rasimaviciute, "Bride to Be Is Stood Up for Her Own Wedding, So She Throws a $35,000 Reception Party for the Homeless Instead," A Plus, October 19, 2015, http://aplus.com/a/wedding-called-off-feast-homeless.

3. "Bono: Action for Africa," YouTube video, 19:55, posted by TED Talks, January 12, 2007, https://www.youtube.com/watch?v=1VOlXwhp00Y.

4. "Franklin Delano Roosevelt Memorial: Quotations," National Park Service, https://www.nps.gov/frde/learn/photosmultimedia/quotations.htm.

5. "Quotes about Hunger," Hunger Hike, http://www.hungerhike.org/quotes -about-hunger/.

6. "Jennifer Aniston," *RGVMag*, http://www.rgvmag.com/features/spotlight /jennifer-aniston/.

Chapter 16 Are You Prepared?

1. Adele R. Cehrs, *SPIKE Your Brand ROI: How to Maximize Reputation and Get Results* (San Francisco: John Wiley & Sons, 2015), 141.

2. "Watch: Dodgers Star Matt Kemp Makes Cancer-Stricken Fan's Day," *CBS News*, May 8, 2013, http://www.cbsnews.com/news/watch-dodgers-star-matt -kemp-makes-cancer-stricken-fans-day/.

3. "Matt Kemp Gives His Jersey to Fan with Cancer," YouTube video, 0:55, posted by G4MarchMadnessHD, August 9, 2013, https://www.youtube.com /watch?v=2r8XNt9UOh8.

4. "Matt Kemp Conversation," YouTube video, posted by Fernanda Souza, May 13, 2013, https://www.youtube.com/watch?v=R93yp15nRCk.

5. Joshua Jones, Instagram post, May 9, 2013, https://www.instagram.com/p /ZBpi6GuR57/.

6. "When Opportunity Comes, It's Too Late to Prepare," Influence Health, http://www.influencehealth.com/insights/blog/when-opportunity-comes-its-too -late-to-prepare.

7. "Hollywood Hero: Mila Kunis Helps Save a Life after Worker Collapses at Her Home," *Daily Mail*, May 8, 2012, http://www.dailymail.co.uk/tvshowbiz /article-2141324/Mila-Kunis-helps-save-mans-life-worker-collapses-home.html.

8. Candice Reed, interview with Dave Donaldson, Springfield, MO, December 2, 2015.

9. Gabrielle Donnelly, "The First Thing I Do Each Day Is Pray," *Catholic Herald*, December 24, 2010, http://www.catholicherald.co.uk/news/2010/12/24 /'the-first-thing-i-do-each-day-is-pray'/.

10. "San Bernardino Shooting: Thousands Mourn at Vigil; 'Let Us Remember,' Mayor Says (Update 3)," *Press Enterprise*, December 3, 2015, http://www.pe.com /articles/community-788123-vigils-san.html.

11. Dominique Mosbergen, "'Random Acts of Pizza' Boston: Reddit, Restaurant Join Forces to Bring Food to Marathon Survivors," *Huffington Post*, April 16, 2013, http://www.huffingtonpost.com/2013/04/16/random-acts-of-pizza-boston -reddit-marathon_n_3094151.html.

Chapter 17 A Vote for Civility

1. Chris Davis, "975 Incredibly Profound Quotes Worth Sharing," Buzzist, January 19, 2016, http://buzzist.com/incredibly-profound-quotes-worth-sharing/.

2. "Nelson Mandela Death: In His Own Words," *BBC News*, December 6, 2013, http://www.bbc.com/news/world-africa-10743920.

3. Beth Chafetz, "Food For Thought," *The Suffield Observer* 17, no. 9 (November 2015): 5.

4. Stephen E. Ambrose, *Nothing Like It in the World: The Men Who Built the Transcontinental Railroad 1863–1869* (New York: Simon and Schuster, 2001), 369.

Chapter 18 Protect and Save

1. Cormac McGee, "Ellen DeGeneres on Radiating Positivity: Shine Bright," Year One, September 10, 2014, http://www.thisisyearone.com/ellen-degeneres -on-positive-energy/.

2. "Information about Sea Turtles: Threats from Marine Debris," Sea Turtle Conservancy, http://www.conserveturtles.org/seaturtleinformation.php?page =marine_debris.

3. Dan Shapley, "Words of Wisdom about the Ocean from Fabien Cousteau, Grandson of Jacques-Yves Cousteau," *Daily Green*, June 3, 2009, http://preview .www.thedailygreen.com/environmental-news/latest/fabien-cousteau-47060302.

4. Calvin B. DeWitt, "Seven Degradations of Creation," in *The Environment and the Christian: What Does the New Testament Have to Teach?*, ed. C. B. DeWitt (Grand Rapids: Baker Books, 1991), 13–23.

5. *Facts and Figures: Managing Water under Uncertainty and Risk*, United Nations World Water Development Report 4, 2012, http://www.unesco.org/new /fileadmin/MULTIMEDIA/HQ/SC/pdf/WWAP_WWDR4%20Facts%20and %20Figures.pdf.

6. United Nations World Water Assessment Programme, *Water and Energy Sustainability: Information Brief*, United Nations, January 2014, http://www .un.org/waterforlifedecade/pdf/01_2014_sustainability_eng.pdf.

7. "About Pick Up America," Pick Up America, http://www.pickupamerica .org/blog#/about/tour.

8. Suzanne Goldenberg and Stephanie Kirchgaessner, "Pope Francis Demands UN Respect Rights of Environment over 'Thirst for Power,'" *The Guardian*,

September 25, 2015, http://www.theguardian.com/world/2015/sep/25/pope-francis
-asserts-right-environment-un.

Chapter 19 Passing Grades

1. "Cerebral Celebs Give Up Screen for Studies," *Fox News*, May 23, 2002,
http://www.foxnews.com/story/2002/05/23/cerebral-celebs-give-up-screen-for
-studies.html.
2. Olivia B. Waxman, "Students Raise Money for Janitor So He Can Visit His
Family Overseas," *Time*, June 6, 2014, http://time.com/2838153/students-raise
-money-for-janitor-so-he-can-visit-his-family-overseas/.
3. Malcolm Gladwell, *The Tipping Point* (Boston: Little, Brown, 2002), 28.
4. "Welcome!," THON: Penn State IFC/Panhellenic Dance Marathon, https://
www.thon.org.
5. "Home," Random Acts of Kindness at UCLA, http://rakatucla.weebly.com.
6. "Welcome to the Random Acts of Kindness Club!," Abraham Lincoln High
School: Random Acts of Kindness Club, http://www.lincolnhigh.net/random
actsofkindness.
7. Dr. Seuss, *The Lorax* (New York: Random House, 1971), 58.

Chapter 20 The Perfect Work Team

1. "MLK Quote of the Week," The King Center, April 9, 2013, http://www
.thekingcenter.org/blog/mlk-quote-week-all-labor-uplifts-humanity-has-dignity
-and-importance-and-should-be-undertaken.
2. Charles Duhigg, "What Google Learned from Its Quest to Build the Perfect
Team," *New York Times Magazine*, February 25, 2016, http://www.nytimes.com
/2016/02/28/magazine/what-google-learned-from-its-quest-to-build-the-perfect
-team.html?_r=0.
3. Cassie Mogilner, Zoë Chance, and Michael I. Norton, "Giving Time Gives
You Time," *Psychological Science* 23, no. 10 (2012): 1233–38, http://www.people
.hbs.edu/mnorton/mogilner%20chance%20norton.pdf.
4. Kevin McClintock, "Charities Team Up with Bass Pro to Help Joplin Families," *Joplin Globe*, October 3, 2012, http://www.joplinglobe.com/news/local_news
/charities-team-up-with-bass-pro-to-help-joplin-families/article_7c1c7439-77f7
-5646-a620-3e47614f5370.html.
5. Rhiannon Williams, "John Sculley: 'Steve Jobs Was Misrepresented in Popular Culture,'" *The Telegraph*, August 30, 2015, http://www.telegraph.co.uk/tech
nology/2015/12/11/john-sculley-steve-jobs-was-misrepresented-in-popular
-culture/.

Chapter 21 Don't Let Go

1. Brandon Specktor, "10 Jane Goodall Quotes That Will Restore Your Faith
in Humanity," *Reader's Digest*, June 2015, http://www.rd.com/culture/jane
-goodall-quotes/.

2. Nolan Moore, "When James Doohan Saved a 'Star Trek' Fan from Suicide," Knowledge Nuts, August 21, 2015, http://knowledgenuts.com/2015/08/21/when -james-doohan-saved-a-star-trek-fan-from-suicide/.

3. *"The Lord of the Rings: The Two Towers*: Quotes," IMDb, http://www .imdb.com/title/tt0167261/quotes.

4. "Exhibitions," The Desmond Tutu Peace Foundation, http://www.tutu foundation-usa.org/exhibitions.html.

Chapter 22 The Decision

1. David Hamilton, *Why Kindness Is Good for You* (Carlsbad, CA: Hay House, 2010), 228.

2. Jamie K. White, "Nurse Picks Up Diner Tab, 46 Others Pay It Forward," CNN, November 7, 2014, http://www.cnn.com/2014/11/06/living/nurse-meal -pay-it-forward/.

3. "24 Teary-Eyed Stories You Must Read about the Touching Kindness of Strangers," *Reader's Digest*, October 2015, http://www.rd.com/true-stories /inspiring/kindness-strangers/.

4. Emma Hogg, "Utah Boy Gets Thousands of Books after Mailman Posts Facebook Plea," *Today*, July 29, 2015, http://www.today.com/news/utah-boy -gets-thousands-books-after-mailman-posts-facebook-plea-t35351.

5. "On the Road: Teen Repays Father's Debt," YouTube video, 1:38, posted by *CBS News*, September 27, 2013, https://www.youtube.com/watch?v=5RYK KqkBK40.

Hal Donaldson has authored thirty books and serves as co-founder/CEO of Convoy of Hope. He has a bachelor's degree in journalism from San Jose State University and a bachelor's degree in biblical studies from Bethany University. He and his wife, Doree, have four daughters.

Kirk Noonan is a former magazine journalist who serves as Vice President of Communications for Convoy of Hope. He has a bachelor's degree in communications from Bethany University and a master's degree in professional writing from Regent University. He and his wife, Janna, have two sons and a daughter.

" SELDOM RESIST THE IMPULSE TO **DO SOMETHING KIND.** "

Hal Donaldson

CONVOY OF HOPE®

WWW.CONVOYOFHOPE.ORG

As a faith-based, nonprofit organization, Convoy of Hope has helped more than eighty million people throughout the world by sharing food, water, emergency supplies, agricultural know-how, and opportunities that empower people to live independent lives, free from poverty, disease, and hunger.

feed ONE

WWW.FEEDONE.COM

feedONE fights hunger and poverty by providing nutritious food and opportunities for children and families in need.

LIKE THIS
BOOK?
Consider sharing
it with others!

- Share or mention the book on your social media platforms. Use the hashtag **#YourNext24**.

- Write a book review on your blog or on a retailer site.

- Pick up a copy for friends, family, or strangers— anyone who you think would enjoy and be challenged by its message.

- Share this message on Twitter or Facebook: **I loved #YourNext24 by @ConvoyOfHope // www.ConvoyOfHope.org @ReadBakerBooks**

- Recommend this book for your church, workplace, book club, or class.

- Follow Baker Books on social media and tell us what you like.

f Facebook.com/ReadBakerBooks

🐦 @ReadBakerBooks